The C[ompassionate]
Inten[tions of Illness]

TONY HUMPHREYS
and
HELEN RUDDLE

Attic

First published in 2010 by Attic Press
Attic Press is an imprint of Cork University Press
Youngline Industrial Estate
Pouladuff Road, Togher
Cork, Ireland

British Library Cataloguing in Publication Data

ISBN-13: 978-0-9552261-9-9

Printed by ColourBooks Ltd., Baldoyle, Co. Dublin
Typeset by Tower Books, Ballincollig, Co. Cork

www.corkuniversitypress.com

Cover image:
'Daffodil II' copyright 2010, David J. Bookbinder (where 2010 is the year
the image was copyrighted, as stated by the Licensor).

I am not a mechanism, an assembly of various sections.
And it is not because the mechanism is working wrongly, that I am ill.
I am ill because of wounds to the soul, to the deep emotional self.
And the wounds to the soul take a long, long time, only time can help.
And patience, and a certain difficult repentance
long, difficult repentance, realization of life's mistake, and the freeing
of oneself
from the endless repetition of the mistake
which mankind at large has chosen to sanctify.

D.H. Lawrence, 'Healing'

We are deeply grateful to all those individuals who shared their stories with us in courageous and open ways. To protect their confidentiality, no one person's story is revealed. The case studies do reflect real lives but are a composite of several stories.

Contents

Introduction:
Everybody Experiences Illness

Illness, death and dying are part and parcel of human life. Despite amazing advances in medical science, there is never going to be a time when we can prevent against ever having the experience of illness. For hundreds of years, men and women of extraordinary ability, creativity, dedication and courage have pursued the quest of discovering the causes and the cures for the most frequent killers of their time. In our own time the quest has focused greatly on cancer, a quest fraught with controversy, contradictions and extremes of optimism and pessimism. There is no question but that these efforts have contributed greatly to the alleviation of human suffering. This book does not belong with the quest for causes and cures – a quest that is properly the domain of medical science – but it does seek to add to the alleviation of the suffering of illness by finding greater understanding of the psychological meaning and purpose of that experience.

Illness, while it manifests physically, also involves deep psychological and social processes on the part of the person suffering the illness. (Illness is also a spiritual process, but exploration of its spiritual dimension is outside the scope of this book.) While we do consider the social processes of illness, to the extent that we consider the personal and professional relationships that surround the person who is ill, the main focus of the book is on the psychological meaning and intent of illness. If, as this book sets out to explore, ways can be found of approaching illness which take compassionate account of the different physical, psychological and social processes that are involved, and ways of responding to those different processes can also be found, then truly great strides will be made in alleviating a suffering that is an all too common experience of human life.

When any one of us becomes ill, we deserve to have all the stops pulled out in our care. Comprehensive care means the institution of appropriate medical care in response to the physical causes and symptoms of illness and, alongside medical treatment, the institution of appropriate psychological care in response to the psychological intentions – the intentions of the self – underlying the illness.

While the alleviation of suffering is a compelling cause, in this book, with its focus on the psychological meaning of illness, we are concerned primarily with a larger process. The larger process involved is the continual impetus of the self towards unconditional love, towards safeguarding wholeness, and towards open, direct, conscious self-expression. Physical 'cure' may, and often does, occur as a result of undergoing this larger process, but it is not the primary focus. As yet, information on the physical 'causes' of illness is limited, but there is even less understanding of the psychological 'intentions' of illness. We seek to contribute to an understanding of the intentions of the self in illness. We recognize that there can be a social reaction to illness which implies that it is a punishment or warning to the ill person from forces outside the person or even from within the person's own body; a reaction that implies that somehow illness reflects badly on the person's level of personal maturity or character, that somehow you 'brought it on yourself', or that the body can somehow 'turn on you' and become your enemy. But in this book we emphasize that 'there is no enemy within', that illness springs from your always wise and compassionate self, that you are not a victim but a powerful and awesome creator in what is often an unsafe psychological environment.

Any reading of medical science literature reveals the enormous complexity, even mystery, of our physical being; this book springs from the recognition of the equally wondrous complexity and creativity of our psychological being. When the self experiences threats to its expression, it creatively uses many canvases, including the body, to reveal and, ultimately, restore wholeness. The book gives the self centre stage. It is the self that orchestrates your responses to your life experiences. The impetus of self is always towards maintaining the place of unconditional love, towards protecting the wholeness of being in whatever ways possible, and towards providing the opportunities for an aware expression of self to emerge. When it becomes dangerous for a person to express an aspect of his or her being, whether as a child or as an adult, the self finds a substitute way to bring attention to that repressed aspect. Among the myriad substitute responses available to the self, illness is one very powerful possibility. The purpose of the illness, as with all substitute responses, is to reduce the threat to well-being (wholeness) that exists and to alert us to the need for that block to expression to be resolved.

Safety is the crucial context for conscious and direct expression of the self in the various forms available to it: physical, emotional, social, behavioural, intellectual, sexual and creative. Illness, as with every human experience, takes place in the psycho-social context of the level of safety that is present in our different worlds – starting with the womb and on to the family, school, community, workplace and wider social systems. In this book we are concerned with the psycho-social contexts within which illness occurs and the creative response of the self to those particular contexts and the threats they pose. We consider illness to have the same fundamental purpose as other psychological and social symptoms – such as depression or aggression or anxiety – which is, in a substitute way, to safeguard the integrity of the self when it is under threat. These symptoms have the further purpose of drawing attention to the real responses that are needed to resolve the existing threats. The combination of psychological safety and real, rather than substitute, action is highly likely to lead to an amelioration of the symptoms, but the larger purpose of the self is to safeguard wholeness.

Joy and well-being, and pain and illness, are part and parcel of being human. There are no human beings who are safe enough always to give expression, consciously and directly, to their amazing and unique self. In truth, we all have experienced threats to our well-being in the different environments in which we operate and, as a result, have repressed many expressions of self. Those expressions of self that have had to be hidden wisely and inevitably reveal themselves in symptoms, these symptoms signifying the underlying issues that require resolution. The symptoms may be physical, psychological or social in nature; generally, a combination of all three. We attempt here to show how illness is no different from other symptoms that alert us to blocks to conscious expression of our true self. In the same way that, for example, depression, chronic anxiety, aggression, addictions, obsessive-compulsive behaviours are very powerful indicators of what lies hidden, so too is illness. The intention of all physical and psycho-social suffering is to protect us from an ever deeper pain – alienation from self – and to alert us to the need to resolve that alienation. It is important that we do not condemn ourselves, or others, when illness occurs. There needs to be compassionate understanding of the fact that, at any time, for any one of us, relieving an illness symptom can present itself as a safer undertaking than to take on the challenge of relieving the darkness of repression of some, or all, expressions of one's true self.

Children, if they have been held with safety in the womb, start out by wonderfully and unconsciously expressing the fullness of their nature. But children encounter adults, who, out of a need to survive, have repressed aspects of their true nature and who, as a consequence, are unable to encourage and celebrate the child's self-expression. The cycle of repression then gets repeated, because it would be highly dangerous for children to maintain spontaneous expression of their nature in the face of threats from significant adults upon whose care they depend. Even as tiny infants, we begin to develop our protectors and defensive strategies in the face of threat; we build up a shadow world behind which our true self lies hidden and protected.

Take the case of the child who presented with recurring vomiting; vomiting that totally stopped when the mother held the child physically close, but would recur when the mother returned to rejecting ways. The vomiting, in a substitute way, served the wise purpose of having the need for emotional nurturance met and it drew attention to the mother's repression of the spontaneous expression of love and its blocking effects on the child. It was not safe for the child to reach up spontaneously to the mother for love; earlier experiences having resulted in a painful non-responsiveness and sometimes harsh rejection. The self of the child, the executor of the child's being, cleverly found an alternative way to draw attention to its need. But compassionate responding to the mother's dark interior world is the ultimate resolution required in such a case of child illness. It is not that the mother deliberately rejected her child; the mother was operating from a place of repression, below consciousness. The child's illness served also as a wise alerting signal for the mother.

The self as creator needs to be understood if we are truly going to reduce further the extent of human suffering. The self is wise, all-seeing, and knows when it is safe for the person 'to be' and when it is safer 'not to be'. The self creates the protectors that are most likely to be powerful in any given situation. It is for this reason that the same illness present today may have a different meaning when it appears at some other time. Furthermore, because each person is unique in his or her experiences of the worlds he or she inhabits, the same symptoms in different people have an individualized meaning; any generalizations, by losing the particular meaning for the individual, miss out on the vital intention of the symptom.

This book provides guidance on how to uncover the particular intentions that your self has when an illness becomes present in your life. The uncovering of intentions is a deep and sensitive process. The process is deep because the roots of the repressions involved are likely to go back a long time to early life. The process is sensitive because it was threat in the first place that led to the repressions. There can be huge sadness when we come face to face with the threats that have been there for us, and the protectors or substitute responses we have had to create to survive. There may be a sense of regret that we have had to use the canvas of the body to bring into the light the pain, unmet needs and disharmonies that have emerged in our lives. Accordingly, the process of uncovering intentions calls out for compassion, patience and loving kindness.

When the self is operating at an unconscious level – which it does when the environment is too unsafe to do otherwise as, for example, in childhood – the language it employs is often metaphorical. There is a great wisdom in the self revealing what it needs to reveal in indirect ways, which are less likely than direct ways to bring further hurt and abandonment. An understanding of the layered meaning of the language used, particularly when the person is describing his or her illness symptoms, helps enormously in uncovering the underlying intentions, and in providing a compassionate response to illness. The location of the illness and the function of the body part in question, along with the person's description of symptoms, often 'spills the beans' on the hidden psycho-social issues that the self, through the illness, is attempting to bring forward into conscious awareness. It is the privileged task of those of us who help others who are suffering to create the unconditional relationship and accompanying profound safety that will enable them to explore the deeper meaning and creative intentions of their illnesses.

From what has been said thus far, it may be clear that while medical professionals are, necessarily, concerned primarily with the causes of illness, psycho-social practitioners are more concerned with the intentions of illness. The intention of the self in illness is to find a substitute way of maintaining wholeness, of offsetting threats to well-being, and of gaining some kind of attention for the hidden hurt that needs to be resolved. A further intention of the self in illness is to alert us to the threats that are present and, when safe, to find real ways of eliminating or reducing those threats. Take the example of the teacher who suddenly falls ill some days before a school inspector is due to carry out an examination of the school's performance. The teacher's illness is real, its cause may be traced to a virus, but its intention may not be uncovered unless the teacher's illness is explored in the context of his present personal and professional worlds. The medical practitioner may effectively prescribe for the presenting physical symptoms, but the possible deeper issues of dependence on approval, fears of failure and criticism, and performance anxiety will continue and become more entrenched, and are likely to reappear, particularly when emotional threats of judgement and criticism and performance demands become present in the teacher's life.

The core of this book is to provide the understanding and guidance that will enable the reader to at least begin to uncover the wise intentions of any illness that may arise in one's life. Further, the book offers guidance for any person in a personal or professional relationship with someone who is ill to provide the safe environment and compassionate responding that make it more likely that the intentions of the illness will indeed be uncovered and resolved.

Medicine does what it does very well. Medical achievements – to mention but very few – include the relief of pain, treatment of infections, the removal of diseased parts of the body, the life-prolonging use of technological aids such as pacemakers, the maintenance of mobility through hip, knee and other replacements, as well as the provision of a range of prostheses used, for example, in limb and breast replacement. If, as this book proposes, illness is a wise manifestation of the shadow world we necessarily have created, the elimination or reduction of illness symptoms plays a very important role in making it physically possible for the ill person to work on the deeper 'dis-ease'. When, for example, you are in the middle of an experience of intense migraine headache, ruptured appendix or severe back pain, it is not possible for you to give consideration to what these symptoms are compensating for or alerting you to resolve. But while relief from the physical experience is necessary, ultimately the healing of illness lies at the deeper psycho-social level. Medicine provides the necessary relief from physical suffering that makes it possible to look at the deeper intentions of the illness. Many medical practitioners recognize that there is a deeper intention in illness and refer the individuals treated by them to psycho-social practitioners, who can assist in uncovering the unique intentions of the illness for the individual concerned. Of course, it is not the remit of the medical professionals to treat blocks to conscious, authentic expression of the self, but they can certainly add to the amazing work they already do by recognizing that illness does have meaning and wise intention.

In order for others to help the ill person to respond to the deeper intentions of his or her illness, it is necessary to have compassionate understanding and to create the physical, emotional and intellectual safety that will enable the person consciously to take up the healing that is being called for. Each one of us wants to be in a conscious place of wholeness and well-being, but unless there is safety for us in our worlds, the self wisely will keep hidden the secrets of the hurts experienced. Patience, too, is essential, since the greater the hurts and abandonment experienced, the greater the fear of ever trusting anybody again. Some individuals have been so cruelly abandoned that giving the psycho-social helper even a glimpse of their real self is far too threatening. These people deserve perseverance in compassionate responding, even though they may not ever feel safe enough totally to avail of such responses from another.

It has to be recognized that professionals involved in any way with illness themselves undergo the very same psychological processes as the person exhibiting the illness. It is for this reason that they need to be provided with the safe opportunities to look to their own inner terrain and their own protectors and substitute behaviours. Sadly these opportunities are not typically provided; this is unfortunate because the interior life of each professional involved will largely determine his or her effectiveness in treating the person who is ill. No matter what model of illness health professionals practise, the nature of their relationship with self and with their clients is a critical factor in the progress of the illness. The book provides guidance to enable care professionals to be mindful of their own relationship with self and to see how, out of that central relationship, they then relate to the person presenting with illness.

Responding to intentions is a loving act and calls out for commitment, open-heartedness and deep compassion. This is a challenge for each one of us, since, at one time or another, each of us will inevitably experience illness. What a challenge also for others in a relationship – personal or professional – with a person presenting with illness! But it is a challenge for which we have everything we need, provided, of course, that we receive the necessary support, guidance, backing and training. Our motivation in writing this book is to contribute to enabling each of us to rise to this challenge.

1 The Self:
The Wise Creator of Illness

Are We Victims or Creators?

An essential question needs to be asked in regard to a human being's presence in the worlds he or she encounters: is the person a victim or a creator? Certainly, to date, disciplines such as medicine, behavioural and cognitive psychology, psychiatry, psychoanalysis and educational psychology have considered the person to be 'a victim' of diseases and sickness, 'conditioned' by his or her environment, 'at the mercy of biological drives', 'a lamb to the slaughter' of biological and chemical imbalances and 'at the beck and call' of his or her unconscious mind. As a result of these viewpoints, what has been rolled out, particularly over the last 100 years, is a huge industry of 'control' therapies, drug therapies and interpretative therapies. None of these approaches asks the person how he or she views his or her illness, or depression or learning difficulty. No meaning is attached to any of the physical, psychological or social symptoms that are presented to the practitioner. The person's symptoms are treated as random, as a nuisance, 'something to be got rid of' or at least reduced. The person is rarely involved in the therapeutic programme, other than having to be convinced that he or she should do as told and take the medicine or treatment regime prescribed. There is no question of the person querying the health professional or educational professional or social professional; in fact, it could be dangerous to do so.

But what if the reality is totally opposite to traditional thinking? What if the human being, rather than being a victim, is a creator who actively creates his or her own particular responses to the various worlds he or she encounters? This is not at all a preposterous suggestion. After all, it is readily observable that each child in a family acts in ways that are very different from his or her siblings and forges a unique relationship with each parent. So many parents say: 'All my children are different, such individuals, even though they were all reared in the same family.' But, of course, they were not all reared in the same family because each child's relationship with his mother and with his father is different to that of a brother or sister. It appears then that children are active in the creation of their own responses to each of their parents' responses to them. This phenomenon is true for all the relationships that an individual child or adult will experience; for example, each student in one class has a different teacher and each employee in one workplace has a different manager/employer. We know, too, that each child learns in his or her own particular way and that each child develops a repertoire of behaviours that clearly marks him or her off, not only from a brother or sister, but from his or her peers.

The creativity of children is visible, not only in their particular ways of responding within the family, but also in the substitute behaviours they develop in order to secure some recognition of their presence. Take, for example, the case of a family with two children, where the condition for recognition was academic success – a condition for a sense of belonging that is not an unusual occurrence in parents' relationships with their children. The older boy was known as 'the genius' and he put huge pressure on himself to meet the unrealistic academic expectations of his parents. The younger brother adopted the opposite strategy and found recognition outside the home by requiring a 'special needs' teacher in school. In the same school where his older brother was deemed to be academically 'gifted', the younger child was seen as educationally 'slow'. Of course, the label of 'slow' provided the younger brother with the wonderful means of reducing his parents' expectations, thereby removing threats of 'not being good enough'. However, he also needed to develop a strategy that would gain him some attraction within the home, particularly from his mother, who herself was addicted to success. The child experienced recurrent infections, requiring antibiotics and necessitating the staying at home from school. Illness was his creative way of getting some tender care from his mother. This pattern of behaviour continued into secondary school and early adulthood, until a medical doctor identified the psycho-social factors that lay behind his illness and referred him for psychological help. His brother continued pressurizing himself academically and became more and more emotionally alienated from himself and socially isolated from others. As a young man he became a high suicide risk. Each boy ingeniously found his own ways to reduce the emotional threats of abandonment that existed within the family. Until it became safe for them to risk being seen for self, rather than for an examination result or for an illness, they wisely held on to their respective creations.

The nature, breadth and depth of that capacity to be uniquely creative are immeasurable and awe-inspiring. It is a capacity that invites us to develop widely different intervention and prevention services for individuals who manifest illness, emotional turmoil, social alienation or spiritual despair – services that seek to work with the creative energies of individuals in distress, whatever the nature of the distress, and that are empowering rather than controlling and disempowering. In recognizing our awesome creative capacity as human beings to manage our worlds, the question arises as to what force there is within us that produces such creativity. The answer is the self. In our attempts to understand the meaning of illness in our lives, the self takes centre stage for our attention.

What is Meant by the Self?

Intuitively, we can have a sense of ourselves as being unique, as being unlike any other; a distinctiveness that cannot be pinned down to anything tangible, such as particular dimensions of our physical appearance, or a particular type of intelligence, or a particular way of behaving, or a particular way of relating, or a particular way of feeling. This sense of distinctiveness is one of the meanings of self, referring to the fact that I am a unique presence in the world, with my own very particular life circumstances, with my own particular way of looking out on the world, with my own particular experience of the world, with my own unique journey in life, with my own particular way of making sense of what my world throws up for me, with my own particular sense of where I am headed for in life. This uniqueness in presence has a physical mirror in the uniqueness of my DNA, and more observably in my fingerprints. My self is unrepeatable.

Intuitively, we also have a sense of something that remains constant in all the passing play of our lives. For example, my feelings come and go, and there is an 'I' that notices the comings and goings; sometimes my behaviour is passive and sometimes it is assertive, and there is an 'I' that notices these different behavioural expressions; sometimes there is confusion in my life and sometimes there is knowing, and there is an 'I' that notices these different intellectual states. This constant 'noticer' is another important dimension of what is meant by the self. The self is the 'Seer', 'Knower', 'Witness' of everything that turns up in my life.

Clearly, the Seer is separate from what is seen, the Knower is separate from what is known and the Witness is separate from what is witnessed. So it can be seen then that the Seer, the Knower, or the Witness, in its separateness, is undiminished, unblemished, untarnished by whatever pain, hurt, suffering turn up in my life and, conversely, is not 'made greater' by any achievements, successes or approval from others that may occur. This untouchable 'wholeness', this inviolate integrity, is a further important dimension of what is meant by the self.

Intuitively, we can also have a sense of ourselves as always 'figuring things out', of 'making our way through' whatever circumstances our lives present to us, of 'seeing how things are and trying to manage as best we can'. This sense of being a 'manager' in our lives is a further important dimension of what is meant by self. The self is the 'Executor' of my life; the self assesses the level of threat present in the different worlds I inhabit and knows when it is safe to take direct action and when it is necessary to use substitute means to safeguard well-being.

The self as unique presence, as Seer, Knower, Witness, as Executor, as inviolate wholeness, is present from the womb. The impetus of the self, from the start in the womb, is towards love. The self knows your worthiness of unconditional love. The place of unconditional love, of giving and receiving love, is a crucial dimension of what is meant by the self. Unconditional love is the lifeblood of the self; love of oneself and love of others. The wisdom of the self is informed by love; it is through love that we wisely know when there is threat in the environment and it is through love that we wisely decide whether to take direct or substitute action to address the threat. It is through love that we seek to create, and are able to create, the safety that will enable us to be open-hearted, non-judgemental, compassionate with others – others who, too, have an inviolate, wise, loving self at the core of their being. The primary process of the self is to try to stay in the place of unconditional love.

Expressions of the Self

In our human existence the self, and the loving energy of the self, is expressed in many extraordinary and wonderfully creative ways through the human capacities available to each and every one of us:

- Physically
- Emotionally
- Socially
- Intellectually
- Behaviourally
- Sexually
- Creatively.

These are means of expression available to the self, but the self is not identified with any one of them; the self is the manager or Executor of these expressions – it observes, bears witness, directs them, and it knows when there can be open and direct expression and when protective expression is the safest option. These different forms of expression are the means by which the self seeks to make its unique presence known, to show its loving nature and to attract and receive love. Particularly as children, we need others around us to understand that our self is separate from these expressions and that we are not loved, for example, on condition that one's self is expressed in a beautiful, strong, healthy body, or on condition that one's self is expressed through the intellectual ability to do well at school, or on condition that one's self is expressed through accommodating, quiet, gentle behaviour. These different forms of expression are here for the loving purposes of the self, for its authentic, real visibility in the world; they are not here to please others, or mind others, or protect others.

Safety in the relationships we experience, from childhood right through to adulthood, is the crucial context for the open, spontaneous, real expression of self. (The nature of psychological safety is discussed more fully in Chapter 2.) The self knows our unconditional worthiness of visibility and love and we start out in life with open, spontaneous, real self-expression. But if in our earlier worlds of womb, family, school and community, our open, real expressions are not spontaneously responded to with love, the self will recognize this dangerous state of affairs and will create substitute means of attracting some level of attention and some semblance of love; because to be completely without love would be the place of despair that we could not survive as children. (These substitute means are discussed more fully in Chapter 3.) The substitute ways that the self wisely creates in circumstances of threat together make up what may be described as a shadow world.

The shadow world of substitute behaviours may be an unreal world created by the self out of the necessity for protection against threat, but, unless the shadow world is understood for what it is, one may live almost wholly from there, leading to an extremely limited existence or ongoing ill health. The challenge lies not in changing our substitute behaviours but in getting to understand them, so that we may bring into the light what they are signifying as lying hidden, and find open, direct, spontaneous self-expression. Our shadow world is not the target for change; we have created it to serve us well. The crucial process is bringing forward and expressing what has had to lie hidden, perhaps for a very long time. If we follow the process of emerging rather than changing, the protective behaviours will have served their purpose and will begin to reduce and eventually disappear.

Your Inner Terrain: The Key to Illness

When the person is viewed as victim, then there can be no explanation as to why some people who smoke heavily get lung cancer while others do not, or why, within a specific community exposed to infection, some people succumb while others do not. But when the individual is seen as creator, then explanations abound for the many variations that occur in experiences of illness. What the creator creates in his or her outer world reflects his or her inner terrain, a terrain that is unique to each person. The inner terrain refers to the level of self-holding that a person has within – his or her level of inner safety. The nature of the inner terrain reflects the extent of repressions of aspects of self that have had to take place and the consequent level of inner discordance. My inner terrain may be more or less conterminous with my shadow world of substitute behaviours, depending on how safe I am in the different worlds I inhabit. If I am very safe, then my inner terrain will closely resemble open, direct, true expression of self, and, conversely, if I am very unsafe, then my inner terrain will reflect my substitute behaviours of my shadow world. (The term 'self-esteem' is often used to describe how I feel in my inner world.)

The heart of illness lies in the state of the person's unique inner terrain and it is this reality that makes it possible to make individual sense and meaning out of the experience of illness. What is taken into this inner terrain – words, actions, feelings, viruses, bacteria, accidents – will not only vary from person to person but, within the person, will vary from two similar events at different times. For example, the influenza I had last month will be different from the one I contract this month. When the individual does not hold – as most of us do not – a consistently solid interiority, an inner stronghold of safety and self-reliance, then variations in his or her inner terrain may be reflected in variations in illness symptoms. Few of us are safe enough to be continuously self-possessed and, as a result, we are often off balance in our inner terrain. The self is aware of, and seeks to redress, the discordance in our inner terrain but knows when it is necessary to use substitute action – such as illness – rather than the more desirable conscious and real means.

Individuals whose expression of self was seriously interrupted necessarily view self-regard, self-expression, self-reliance and self-care as highly threatening and uncomfortable responsibilities. Wisely, they will not move from their protective, substitute shadow world until they encounter ongoing compassion, belief in their limitless capacity, patience and support. Any of us in the health-care professions need to be ready to enter into a relationship with individuals who seek our help, and need to be in a position to foster hope rather than hopelessness, through recognizing the wise and compassionate meaning of illness in the context of the person's inner terrain.

The concept that the key to illness lies in the state of one's inner terrain is not new. In the nineteenth century the noted physician Claude Bernard wrote: 'illnesses hover constantly about us, their seeds blown by the wind, but they do not set into the terrain unless the terrain is ready to receive them'. Louis Pasteur, the father of microbiology, agreed with Bernard when he exclaimed on his deathbed: 'the germ is nothing; the terrain is all'. The understanding of the role of 'the terrain' in illness was taken to a deeper level by Georg Groddeck (Groddeck, 1977), humanitarian physician and psychoanalyst, recognized as the father of psychosomatic medicine. Speaking of the creativity of illness, Groddeck's language is poetic:

> . . . we still pretend that illness is an evil, as if the self weren't as
> sublime in the language of illness as it is in the language of art or
> poetry or researching. We still do not understand that in the illness

the self expresses thoughts as deep as in the gospels and that it announces in both forms the very same things: 'Behold the greatness of God and the miracle of man!'

Groddeck spells out clearly that illness is meaningful: 'Illness does not come from the outside; it is not an energy but a creation of the self. The self tries to express something by illness – to be ill has to mean something.'

It is possible, then, to view illness, not as tragedy, nor as a fault in us, but as an awesome creation of the self. Illness is an opportunity created by the self to manifest what lies hidden in the shadow world, so that we can consciously get back on the psycho-social well-being path. The illness symptoms provide the prompt to look deeper at the state of one's inner terrain, so that the disharmony that exists may be healed and there may be open, free expression of self. It must be acknowledged that such an undertaking is not easily done in a world where it is often dangerous to be real, authentic and true to one's self. Safety is the essential ground that will enable individuals to reveal their true selves and, in so doing, have less need of illness as a substitute means of obtaining some level of recognition. It can be seen, then, that the nature of the relationships surrounding the person experiencing illness needs mindful attention. (This topic is discussed more fully in Chapter 9.)

Illness: One Indicator of the State of Your Inner Terrain

How we are within ourselves may be mirrored by the self in our bodies; but it must be emphasized there is not always a direct correspondence between the two. When I am perfectly at peace and at one with self, this oneness may be embodied as physical wellness or well-being. But, of course, there could also be the case that, because I am elderly, my physical functioning has deteriorated but, in my inner terrain, I am at peace and true to self. It could also be the case that my inner terrain is very much off balance but my self chooses a canvas other than the body – for example, the behavioural symptom of aggression – to draw attention to the turmoil within me, and I may remain perfectly well in my body. The body is not the only means by which the self manifests the state of my inner terrain but it is a very powerful means of manifesting inner disconnection and of attempting to correct it, albeit at a physical and substitute level.

The wise intent of the self is that this embodying through illness of the inner conflict will draw attention to the real psychological and social actions being called for. When the person experiencing illness is in an unsafe world and, as a result, cannot attend to the deeper meaning of the illness embodiment, the symptoms are likely to intensify or certainly recur. While this book does not ignore the fact of physical causes of illness – such as viruses, trauma, genetic make-up, environmental triggering agents – that are connected with our physicality as human beings, it concerns itself with the psycho-social intentions of any particular illness. Because the illness reflects the unique inner terrain of the individual, the same illness symptom, such as migraine headache, in several individuals has a particular intention for each person so afflicted. Similarly, the recurrence of the same illness in a particular person may well have a different intention at the different times it manifests itself.

It is not just the embodiment itself that brings crucial information on one's inner terrain; dimensions of illness – such as intensity and frequency – are important mirrors of the seriousness of the inner turmoil. The duration of the symptoms also often functions as a mirror of the extent of the inner disconnection. Consideration of all the circumstances surrounding the illness can give further valuable information on the deep healing intentions of the illness.

The location of the illness is an important source of information on its deeper intention. (The significance of location is discussed more fully in Chapter 5.) Is the embodiment located in the sense organs (perhaps, calling for 'sense' to be made of the symptoms or for 'common sense')? Is it located in the support organs (perhaps alluding to the need to be more 'supportive' or 'definite' with oneself and others)? Is the embodiment located in the vital organs, such as the heart, the lungs, the liver, the kidneys, the brain (perhaps calling for critical and 'deep-seated' issues to be realized and resolved)?

Consideration of the inner and outer circumstances that form the context in which the illness appears is critical to getting to the inner turmoil that has become embodied. The inner world of thoughts, images, dreams, memories that were there *before* the onset of the illness, as well as those thoughts, feelings, dreams and images that accompany the embodiment, is often a valuable source of enlightenment. The person's outer life circumstances – for example, family life, intimate relationships, crises, career and relationships at work – are further significant sources of information as to the intentions of the self in the illness.

Responding to the Inner Terrain: The Key Response to Illness

The self's capacity to employ the canvas of the body creatively – as a substitute way of drawing attention to the lack of unconditional love and consequent interruption of the expression of aspects of self – means that it is the inner terrain that needs to be the primary focus of the person experiencing the illness and that needs to be a central consideration for any health professionals involved with the person. Medical interventions that eliminate or reduce the physical symptoms play a very important role in making it physically possible for the person to work on the deeper 'dis-ease' in the inner terrain. For the person in great physical pain or discomfort, it is not possible to focus on the state of his or her inner terrain and to give consideration to what hidden issues he or she may be trying to bring into the light through his or her illness symptoms. Medicine provides the necessary relief from physical suffering that makes it possible to look at the deeper intentions of illness. Ultimately, the issue is not about 'cure'. Illness is about *realization* – making real what has been hidden behind the substitute psychological, social and physical symptoms. The professional response needed to illness is about creating the safe holdings (see Chapter 2) to enable conscious, open and free expression of the self. When there is greater safety for the

self to directly seek what is needed for its well-being, illness will not be needed to the same extent, and the self will be better able to return the body to its state of well-being.

2 Safe Holding for Open
Self-Expression

Safety: A Crucial Issue for Adults, as for Children

The safety to be self, to give open and spontaneous expression to self, and to operate out freely from our unique nature is critical to our well-being as individuals and as a collective of individuals. Safety is the critical ingredient in any relationship, not just between parents and children but also between teachers and students, partner and partner, employer and employee, and employee and fellow-employee. While there has been a developing consciousness of the crucial importance of creating safety in the rearing of children, particularly physical and sexual safety, and to some extent emotional safety – prompted, perhaps, in part by shocking revelations of violations in these human expressions – there has not been a corresponding realization of the need for safety in relationships between adults. But violations can occur in all relationships and can involve any of the means of expression available to us as human beings: physical, sexual, emotional, social, intellectual, behavioural and creative. For example, one of the most common complaints of employees is that they feel anonymous at work, and a frequent experience of students is that academic performance is considered more important than they themselves.

Safety is a serious issue, because when safety is lacking in marriages and partnerships, in adult relationships within communities, within the workplace, within educational institutions, within healthcare systems, the consequences in terms of human misery can be overwhelming. This is so because when safety is not present for an adult, or for a child, then the self creatively finds ways to reduce the threats to its well-being; for example, through the substitute behaviours of avoidance, aggression, manipulation, control, passivity, absenteeism, physical withdrawal, emotional withdrawal, and a myriad of other substitute ways of being in an unsafe world. (Substitute behaviours are described in detail in the next chapter.)

The Meaning of Safety

Safe holding is the crucial context for open, spontaneous, real expression of your self in the different capacities available to you: physical, sexual, emotional, social, intellectual, behavioural and creative (the nature of safe holding in these different domains of expression is described in succeeding sections in this chapter). Safe holding is essentially about the need to be loved unconditionally and to love unconditionally. Unconditional love is our core energy, all-encompassing and not to be confused with the romantic feelings often referred to as 'love' in romantic literature or music. The self deserves to be loved unconditionally, and any identification of the self with any particular expression profoundly threatens the impetus of the self to love and be loved. Unconditional love creates the safe-holding ground for the self to be free to express its wholeness.

In order to maintain the spontaneous, free-flowing impetus of love, the self needs safe holding – unconditionally loving holding – in each of the worlds you inhabit in your life. The first world you inhabit is the womb; at this stage the womb being your world (womb-world). As you go through life, you inhabit further worlds; the family being a critical world in infancy and childhood and, in later childhood, school and community becoming other major worlds. Further worlds are formed by the workplace and the wider social systems in which you participate. In the case of the child, adults necessarily have the responsibility to create the safe holding – a human reality that, sadly, carries its own tragedies, since the adults in our childhoods are not often in a position to provide the safe holding needed. But in adulthood we need to, and can, take on ourselves the responsibility for our own safe holding – and, in truth, can make a much better job of it than any other person could, since we are privy to information that nobody else could have on the state of our inner world.

It is the nature of human existence that for long periods of life, all during childhood, we are completely dependent for our survival on the adults around us, most particularly our parents. As a child, you need to be able to attract the adults in your life in order to have any degree of security. If your spontaneous, real self-expressions attract unconditional loving, then your world is wonderfully safe and you can be self-possessed and free. But, of course, none of us, as children, has had completely safe holding in our worlds; it is not possible, because we are born to human parents who themselves have not been held with complete unconditional love and are operating from their own shadow worlds. In adulthood, while we still need, and deserve, safe holding in our worlds, if we are not received by others with unconditional love, we now, unlike in childhood, have the possibility of taking care of ourselves; we can openly maintain our sense of worthiness, and we can actively and directly seek out what we deserve.

While none of us is ever met with consistent and persistent unconditional love, it is also true that very few of us experience complete lovelessness. What we usually experience is a mixed bag of loving and abandonment within any particular relationship in whatever environment that relationship occurs. When 'good enough' – a term coined by the psychologist D. W. Winnicott (Winnicott, 1965) – parenting, teaching, managing, caring are present, we have enough safety to hold on to our true selves. 'Good enough' is a wonderful term because neither children nor adults expect us to 'get it right' all the time, to be in the open, real place all the time. However, even 'good enough' relating is not very common and there are few of us who have not experienced psychological threats that lead to us wisely repressing those aspects of self that were experienced as triggering harsh and unloving responses.

As already described, the self manifests its nature in several ways – physically, emotionally, sexually, intellectually, behaviourally, socially and creatively. For each of those expressions of self there needs to be a corresponding safety. The nature of the safe holding required in these different domains of expression is discussed in the following sections of this chapter. While the self has these expressions, it is not identifiable with these expressions; the self is indivisible. The self is the Executor and will manage/execute these expressions when safety is present. When there is safety, the creation of a substitute world is not required. Safety, then, needs to be established not only for children and adults to express their difference and uniqueness, but to bring forward the fullness of their human nature across the range of human expressiveness.

Safe Holding for Physical Self-Expression

It is important to understand that the self has a body, but the self is not the body. If I become identified with my body – the 'body beautiful' or the 'body ugly' – then the body becomes a substitute means of attracting the love that is deserved for self. I may be obsessed with 'looking good' in order to be seen, or I may avoid intimacy with others because of feeling 'ugly and unwanted'. Of course, the body is hugely important as our means of experiencing the world. The self needs the body to be healthy, but health is not its priority; wholeness is. When wholeness is threatened, the self will work through the body as a substitute means of protecting its wholeness; illness being one such substitute means. Illness is not the threat; the threat lies in wholeness not being held. Even as a foetus in the womb, we powerfully express our physical needs. Frank Lake (Lake, 1966), a pioneer in the study of the life of the human being in the womb, believes that there is an individual present at the moment of conception and that parenting of that unique individual needs to start at this point, not at birth, as many people would have thought.

Abraham Maslow (Maslow, 1954), a psychologist who is well known for his work in charting the hierarchy of human needs, emphasizes that the physical needs of the infant are the most urgent ones. Among the infant child's physical needs are the needs to be held, to be warm, to be safe from any physical threat, to be fed, for thirst to be quenched, to move, to touch, to urinate, and to defecate.

Later on, the child needs to learn to feed itself, to walk, to take charge of his or her own bodily functions, to check out his or her physical world. Of course, the meeting of the child's physical needs is a basic dimension of the creation of safe physical holding, but the emotional tone in which the physical needs are responded to is the critical dimension of safety. The importance of the emotional relationship was starkly highlighted in the case of the thousands of orphaned Romanian children who, while physically cared for, were otherwise left unattended and lay immobile in row after row of cots, with no child reaching up for nurturance. Some older children's legs were crippled because they could not stretch. After weeks of warm holding, feeding, caring and playing, the younger children's hands reached up when care workers came by. It took the older children considerably longer before they reached up again.

The adults in the child's life need to convey unequivocally that the child's body is sacred, always deserving of respect, honouring and dignity. An important way of conveying this message is how the child is held physically; when held with affection, tenderness, respect and care, when cuddled, kissed, massaged, rubbed and stroked, this conveys to the child the rightness of his or her particular body. When the child's physical needs are met with loving kindness, and his or her physical presence is held with unconditional love, then that child is free to engage in open, spontaneous, physical self-expression. Any impatience, roughness, ignoring, slapping, shouting, irritability, aggression or invasion will lead to repressions of the particular expressions that were punished. Clearly, the frequency and severity of the defensive responses experienced will have a telling effect on the level of repression and the kinds of substitute behaviours that the self has to develop. Illness is one of the myriad substitute responses that the self may create in the face of such threats to physical self-expression.

A second very important dimension of the creation of safe physical holding is concerned with the cherishing of the person's unique physical appearance. Comparisons pose grave threats to our physical self-expression; a reality to which one of the present author's

experience bears testimony when, right into adulthood, he was protectively very rejecting of his physical appearance as a result of being
compared to his 'good-looking' brother, and his serious doubts about
his attractiveness led him to avoid intimate relationships for many
years. The rise in anorexia nervosa among young women, and an
alarming increase in the occurrence of the same embodiment in
young males, point to serious threats around physical appearance in
homes, schools and communities, and in the wider society. We need
to have the message strongly conveyed to us that 'your body is here
for you; it is your vehicle for exploring and living in the world; and
your body is fundamentally right in itself'. The appearance of one's
body is not the measure of its value; that value is a given.

A third dimension of the creation of safe physical holding is
having the knowledge you need on how your body operates. With
this knowledge, you can learn how best to care for your body; you
can become practised in tuning into your bodily experiences; you
can learn to enjoy your body and be appreciative of the pleasures
and experiences it enables you to have.

Safe Holding for Sexual Self-Expression

The self has sexual energy, but is not its sexuality. Sexuality is an
energy, a life force that is present in us, irrespective of our sexual
activities. Sexual expression may involve the immense pleasure to be
had from the pleasuring of oneself or another and from sexual intercourse, but it is a threat to our sexual safety to enmesh sexuality with
sexual activity. It is also a serious threat to our sexual safety to
enmesh our sexuality with our physical appearance; a threat that is
very prevalent in current society, where the message is strong that
sex is only for the beautiful, only for those whose bodies match up
to the standards laid down by the media and commercial interests.

There is an urgent need for recognition of the fact that infants and
toddlers are sexual beings and, at the other end of the scale, pen-
sioners and senior citizens are also sexual beings. The behavioural
expression of that sexual energy needs to be appropriate to where we
are in our lives. As children, we need the safety of not being exploited

by adults to engage in sexual activity that is right for adults. As older people, we need the safety to be respected and honoured in our continued desire for, and interest and participation in, sexual activity. There is a need, too, for the safety to choose what kind of activity (if any) fits for us (once it does not pose any threat to the sexual boundaries of another person) and to choose what sexual orientation is right for us. The decision not to be sexually active does not mean that you are not sexual; there needs to be the safety of having that decision recognized. Such a safety may be very important in the lives of teenagers and young adults. The message needs to be strongly conveyed that 'your sexuality belongs to you; it's here for you, for your fulfilment, for your pleasure and for you to experience connection with another; it is your choice how you express that sexuality.

Infants and toddlers quickly discover their erogenous zones; this, more often than not, is a source of embarrassment to those adults who have not resolved their own sexual repressions. How adults respond to children's sexual explorations is critical to whether or not children will continue to give open, spontaneous expression to their sexuality. Of course, children need to be warmly guided on the appropriateness of privacy when sexually pleasuring themselves and they need to learn to respect the sexual boundaries of other children and, indeed, of adults. However, adults need to be vigilant about their non-verbal communication – a look of disgust is quickly detected by infants and children, who are experts at reading faces. Religions have not served human sexual expression very well by their fear, and resultant condemnation, of normal sexual practices. The repressions and substitute behaviours that were created in response to a dark religious history of demonizing sexuality are numerous. Some examples are guilt, scruples, shame, sexual abuse, asexuality, perversions, fetishisms, impotency, promiscuity and fear. If religion was, and still is in many cases, a dark force that threatens human sexual expression, in contemporary society the pornography industry has objectified sexuality and reduced it to outward physical appearances and, as a result, is threatening its capacity for emotional and spiritual union with self and with another.

Openness, celebration and knowledge are the key holding responses required so that sexual expression does not become sexual repression. Ignorance is not bliss when it comes to sexuality. There is a tendency to confuse innocence with ignorance, but whereas innocence means freedom from guilt, ignorance means lack of safety through lack of knowledge.

The lack of a safe holding by adults of children's sexual expression leads to sexual repressions that can later be manifested in such substitute behaviours as fear of sexual intimacy, guilt about self-stimulation, frigidity, potency difficulties, and the use of sexuality as a means to an end. Illness is also one of the many possible substitute behaviours created by the self in the face of threats to sexual self-expression.

Sexual activity, or the lack of it, can be a medium for other emotional repressions to manifest themselves. Sexual protective behaviours may represent fear of intimacy or fear of emotional rejection. It has been suggested that at least 60 per cent of sexual difficulties between couples reflect deeper relationship issues that need resolution, while another 30 per cent are related to repressions in childhood in response to some violation or sexual punitiveness by an adult, older child or adolescent. When children possess little power in relationships, they may protectively and, of course, unconsciously, use sexual activity as a means of having power over adults – for example, children can be coquettish and act in a seductive manner. The use of sex as a weapon, and as a means to an end, is very prevalent in adult relationships. It is only through compassion, non-judgement and understanding that we can begin to create the safety that is essential for mature sexual expression to go unhindered.

Safe Holding for Emotional Self-Expression

The self has emotions but is not its emotions; 'I have feelings but I am not my feelings'. The separation of self from feelings means that it becomes possible to see your feelings, say, of joy or terror, from above and thereby not become identified with them. When you cannot find that space between the self and the emotion, then you become overwhelmed by the emotion and lose the freedom to respond to it in an open, conscious manner. On the other hand, when we see the self as the creator, it becomes possible for us to notice, regulate, take due action on or transcend the feelings that arise in us.

Our feelings are the truest barometer of how we are doing in our lives. Welfare feelings – for example, contentment, excitement, peace, pleasure, joy, confidence – indicate that there is harmony in our inner terrain. Emergency feelings – for example, hurt, anger, disappointment, fear, depression, loneliness, guilt – come from the self to give warning that threats to our well-being are present, that something is amiss that needs to be attended to before we can move on. Our emotions represent a valuable store of information that is there to serve our well-being. But we need safety to have access to and to use the powerful information our emotions contain. Whether feelings are of an emergency or a welfare nature, it is crucial that children be helped to identify and express what is happening within them. So often we are led to believe that our emotions are irrational, that they can overwhelm us if we 'give into them', that they can get in the way of intelligent action, and that they are meaningless intrusions from outside ourselves. Children frequently get the messages: 'don't feel what you are feeling'; 'don't feel too deeply'; 'don't be so intense'; 'feelings are dangerous'; 'feelings can lead to you being out of control'; 'you are weak when you show feelings'. But, of course, emotions do not disappear because we are told not to have them. In present-day Irish society we are faced with the tragic situation that many young men, rather than talking out what is happening to them emotionally, will take their lives because the risk of emotional expression is too great. Young women and girls are not immune either from emotional threats and in fact self-harm seven times more than their male counterparts; drug-overdosing, for example, representing the swallowing down of their emotional pain, and the cutting of themselves representing the emotional wounds they are not daring to express.

Feelings creatively arise from the self; they are there to give expression to needs or the reality of unmet needs. When children or adults repress or suppress their feelings in a creative response to the dangers of emotional expression, these buried feelings will find some substitute means of expression – substance addictions, or emotional or violent outbursts that appear to come from nowhere, apathy, depression, lifelessness and hysterical behaviour. Illness is one of the substitute behaviours that the self may create in the face of threats to emotional self-expression.

Because emotional literacy is fundamental to well-being, it is the responsibility of adults to seek such literacy, so that, in turn, they can create safe emotional holding for children, adolescents, and indeed for other adults; the safe holding that enables individuals to express feelings, both welfare and emergency. It is the modelling of emotional maturity that particularly provides the permission for children to be expressive of their inner emotional worlds.

Safe Holding for Intellectual Self-Expression

The self has intelligence, but it is not its intelligence. Intelligence provides an amazing means for the self to explore and understand the world you have been born into. The creation of the safe holding for intellectual expression is absolutely necessary for individuals to feel empowered, 'response-able', and thereby responsible.

Most toddlers – if the womb has been a safe world for them – are naturally curious, love learning, have an eagerness to know, and are risk-takers and adventurers. But, as adults, how many of the qualities of the toddler do we now possess? Threats to intellectual expression can abound in the relationships surrounding the child – impatience, irritability, ridicule, scolding, anxiety, crossness, superiority, helplessness, failure to provide opportunities to explore limitless potential, lack of interest, making comparisons with others, having unrealistic expectations, punishment of failure, over-rewarding of success and labelling a child as 'slow', 'weak', 'average', 'stupid', 'dull' and, equally threatening, labelling as 'cleverer' than his or her peers, 'gifted' or 'genius' based on performance in a particular field of knowledge. All human beings are innately intelligent but the stark reality is that much of our intelligence goes into creating substitute behaviours to offset threats, not just to the expression of our amazing intelligence but also to threats in the other domains of expression that are available to us. It is of note that only 3 per cent of so-called 'gifted' children make any important intellectual and social contribution as adults. Sadly, because these children became identified with their high intellectual performance, they lost out on the development of competence in the emotional, social, recreational, creative and spiritual areas of human functioning, which are essential to maturity.

The main threats to intellectual expression are:

- The absence of belief in our intelligence beyond measure – for both children and adults.
- The confusion of intelligence with knowledge.
- The punishment of failure and the over-rewarding of success.
- The identification of the person's worth with an examination result.
- The failure to recognize that each person expresses his or her individuality by being attracted to his or her own preferred area of knowledge.
- The failure to appreciate that each of us learns in our own particular way.

There are few adults who believe in their limitless intelligence and, in turn, they do not show belief in children's intellectual potential – an omission that leads to repression or suppression of intellectual ability. In particular, the confusion of knowledge with intelligence has created a major lack of safety, preventing many people from taking intellectual risks. They know from experience that they will be intellectually judged on what they say or do, and so, wisely, they do not take that risk. Some 70–80 per cent of adults go for the average in terms of achievement, thereby reducing the performance expectations of the significant others in their lives. The mature parent and teacher know that failure and success are intrinsic to learning. But the tragedy is that these two essential learning processes have become extrinsic forces, signalling the end of learning as the adventure it deserves to be. The fear of failure and the addiction to success are two of the more common substitute responses to threats to intellectual expression. In truth, it is difficult to find adults who can hold failure and success as inseparable partners in the wonderful process of acquiring knowledge.

When suicide occurs, it is not uncommon that it follows an examination result; tragically, the person who took his or her life somehow felt that the result that was 'not good enough' equalled his or her being 'not good enough'. No person is an examination result. The significance that adults attach to scholastic attainment and examination results is perceived accurately by children as a great threat to their well-being. Nowadays, children as young as six and seven years complain that they are 'stressed out' by tests; the stress being a powerful substitute response to threat. It should be shouted from the rooftops: 'No person is an examination result.' Illness is one of the many substitute responses that can be created by the self in the face of threats to intellectual self-expression.

The fact that children will often cleverly choose to focus on an aspect of knowledge that is the diametric opposite of that chosen by siblings is often missed by parents and teachers – another serious omission and one that leads to conformity being demanded rather than the appreciation and enablement of individuality. There are some 100 different fields of knowledge and each person needs to be encouraged and supported to follow those knowledge fields that attract them. Interestingly, when adults acknowledge and support the child's individuality, as this is expressed in his or her selection of knowledge fields, he or she is more likely also to take on challenges in other areas of life. However, when the opposite occurs, the child may protectively cease to be motivated to learn, or he or she may conform out of fear but will harbour buried resentment that will erupt some time in the future.

A further example of a common threat to our intellectual expression is the failure to recognize that each person has his or her own preferred way of learning. Whether in the classroom, the lecture room or the training course, each learner has a different teacher. Each learner hears the teacher in a different way and the parent, teacher or trainer who treats all the learners in the same way poses a great threat to their intellectual expression.

The increasing of knowledge and skills can be a never-ending excitement; not knowing or not having a particular skill need to be seen as a challenge and not the embarrassment it has become for so many of us. There needs to be an absence of any threats, as well as the presence of belief, encouragement, excitement, humour and fun, and the assurance that the unconditional loving relationship will not be jeopardized by the pursuit of knowledge.

Safe Holding for Behavioural Self-Expression

As human beings, we have the capacity to develop a highly complex repertoire of behaviours, but while the self has this capacity, the self is not its behaviour. Any confusion of the self with behaviour poses a grave threat and leads to all sorts of creative attempts on the part of the self to protect wholeness – for example, compulsions, obsessions, avoidance, rebelliousness, addiction to success, and manipulation. Illness is also one of the myriad substitute responses created by the self in the face of threats to behavioural self-expression.

A key element in the creation of safe holding for behavioural expression is the understanding that all human behaviour, no matter how frightening, despicable and dark it may be at times, makes sense. Unless we attempt to explore the sense of human behaviour, we cannot make progress in resolving behaviours that threaten the well-being of ourselves and/or others. The categorical judgement of certain behaviours as 'negative' without any attempt to understand their underlying purpose poses a threat and serves only to increase their occurrence. There is no record of any infant who has emerged from the womb suicidal, vicious, threatening, aggressive, manipula- tive, passive, obsequious, or violent. It is the quality of relationships that determines the emergence of such powerful protective responses. These substitute behaviours are not the products of faulty genes, biochemical imbalances or genetic predispositions; these responses arise in relationships and can be transformed in relationships. Individuals do not intentionally make life difficult for others. The hope underlying the creation of any substitute behaviour is that somebody will see what needs to be seen. Sadly, because of the dark inner terrain of adults within many families, schools and communities, and within the health-care professions, these cries for help are often undetected. Troubling or challenging behaviours are best seen as creations, and when they are understood as such and treated with patience and compassion in the context of an unconditional relationship, there is hope that their message will be taken up and resolved.

A further element of safe holding is the recognition of individuality. Each child in a family will ingeniously develop a repertoire of behaviours different from those of his or her siblings. The purpose is to express one's individuality in a behavioural way. Adults who encourage the child in his or her particular behavioural expression support the emergence of the child's individuality. Any criticizing, comparing, diminishing or ridiculing will create a profoundly unsafe holding for the child and will disempower him or her from expressing his or her individuality. The child may conform (act-in) and become ever so obedient, pleasing, perfectionist in his or her behaviour, or he or she may rebel (act-out); either way, the child is now using behavioural substitutes to draw attention to his or her individuality.

What is often not recognized is, that praise focused on the person and not on the specific behaviour in question – 'good girl' or 'great man' or 'you're the best' – poses threat and leads to profound insecurities. Confusion of person with behaviour leads to the protective substitute behaviours of always having to prove yourself through your behaviours and now there is no joy in these behaviours any more. Praise needs to be attached to a specific behaviour – 'thank you for calling when you said you'd call'; 'I can see a lot of effort in this essay and it is a wonderful piece of writing'. Affirmation is for the person, the self, and is not conditional on behaviour: 'I am really happy to see you in my surgery today', or 'you're so special to me'.

Just as praise needs to be targeted at specific behaviour and not at the person, so too correction of behaviour that is threatening, offensive or troubling needs to be targeted at the behaviour and not the person. There are no bad children and no bad adults, but there are behaviours that can seriously threaten the well-being of others. It needs to be recognized that these threatening behaviours themselves arose in response to threatening behaviours and the vicious cycle is likely to continue if the nature of correction is judgemental, punishing and condemnatory. Of course, strong boundaries are required around the protective behaviours of others, but boundaries are established through us taking actions for ourselves and not against those perpetrating the threatening behaviours. For example, in response to an aggressive approach by another, you can create a boundary by asserting: 'I understand that you are feeling angry but I do not respond to being spoken to in an aggressive way and am prepared to listen when you are ready to ask for what you want in a way that is respectful of yourself and of me.' When a child, for instance, spills his milk, the safe holding response is to say, 'I would like you to hold the cup more firmly the next time', not 'You're a bold boy'.

The key elements in the creation of safe holding of the self's behavioural expression are:

- Encouragement
- Focus on effort rather than performance
- Learning from mistakes and failures
- Not getting caught up in success
- Modelling by adults of self-reliance and self-responsibility
- Creation of age-appropriate opportunities for individuals to explore and understand the world they live in and to learn to stand on their own two very capable feet.

Safe Holding for Social Self-Expression

The self seeks to belong, but is not this belonging. Wisely, the self seeks to belong to a parent, a family, a classroom, a school, a community, a workplace, a country. This drive to belong is an attempt to find safety to be oneself in the outer world and, depending on the nature of the holding received, particularly in infancy and early child-hood, the self will set about belonging in either a real or a substitute manner. From the moment of conception, the individual exists in the worlds of other people. The first world is the womb – which is the only world for the foetus – where the manner in which the foetus is received and held is central to its well-being. The family is the second social system that forms a world for the child, and soon afterwards the child becomes exposed to the community as womb-world. In adolescence the wider society as womb-world is opened up to the young person and the myriad tasks of becoming adult poses a serious agenda. Young adulthood is about realizing the self as womb-world; the conscious living out from the place of interiority of the self is the responsibility of the adult. This latter process is made easier when the person's social context provides the kind of holding where it matters whether the person is present or absent in the social situation; for example, the school child needs to know that it matters to his or her teacher and to his or her classmates whether he or she is in the class-room or absent from school.

Tragically, more often than not we experience threats to our wanting to belong, these threats arising primarily from relationships where there was either an over-belonging or an under-belonging, or utter abandonment owing to no belonging.

Over-belonging refers to relationships, within the family or mar-riage or classroom or school or church or workplace, where everything is done for the person and any attempt to challenge this suffocating of individuality can result in harsh emotional rejection. Such relationships tend to be established by adults who have an overwhelming need to be needed (in itself a powerful substitute behaviour) and who become terribly threatened when any member of the social system asserts independence.

Under-belonging refers to the kind of social systems where members are seen as being there for the system in question and they dare not challenge this system. This social system is characterized by dominance and high demands for conformity to the 'should's and 'have to's of the system. Under-belonging poses grave threats of being criticized and exiled for the person who is a member of this highly controlling system. In such a social system, particularly in the family, children will wisely conform (a strong substitute response) and will tailor their lives to fit the demands and commands of the system. In doing so, they protect themselves from further blows to their sacred presence. Other children will rebel and attempt to counter-control, this also being a powerful substitute response whose intention is to force the system to do things for them that they really need to do for themselves. Illness is also one of the possible substitute creations of the self in situations of over-/under-belonging.

There is no darker place than the social system where you experience anonymity or major violations of your presence. Despair is likely to arise here, unless the person manages to find very powerful substitutes such as drugs, alcohol, violence, profound dependence and helplessness or serious illness. At an unconscious level the self realizes that any acting on the drive to belong would be high risk. Tremendous and enduring social safe holding would need to be created in order to entice the person who has been so wounded to emerge from the shadows of addictive or other powerful substitute responses. As long as the protective responses serve the purpose of maintaining some sense of wholeness, they will be creatively held on to. However, if they were to lose that power, then the ultimate protective behaviour may need to be employed – life-threatening illness or suicide – to end the pain of having no safe place to lay one's head.

When the need to belong is responded to in a real and open way, such that the person feels unconditionally seen for self, it becomes possible to use one's full capacity for social expression. The self is always whole and entire in itself but, especially as infants, children and adolescents, we need safe holding in order that the conscious expression of our wholeness can emerge. The young person intuitively knows that he or she is dependent (not helpless!) on the significant social systems in which he or she participates for the meeting of vital needs – family, nursery school, classroom and community. The adult is not necessarily in that dependent position and, even when he or she is, he or she can free himself or herself of the social system's ties that bind and become independent. In practice, this process of becoming adult – self-reliant – is made considerably easier where there are social systems that support that maturing process. While it is the responsibility of each person to become adult, individuals in leadership roles have a particular responsibility to create environments that foster social safety for social belonging.

The social valuing and acceptance of another person do not mean putting up with behaviours that are hurtful or demeaning of your presence. On the contrary, creating social safety involves taking strong action to assert your dignity, but in a way that is open and does not jeopardize the valuing relationship with the other. Judgement, control, narcissism and passivity are examples of protective substitute behaviours developed in the face of social threats that, in turn, create social threat for others. Understanding, empathy, assertiveness, supportiveness and authenticity constitute the key elements in the creation of safe holding for social belonging and social expressiveness.

Safe Holding for Creative Self-Expression

Each of us is working out our own unique life-path; each of us is constantly devising creative strategies for dealing with the particular circumstances that our particular lives have thrown up for us. We are always actively engaged with our lives; whether this be in an open and real or a substitute and protective manner. We will engage with life in an openly creative way if we have the safety to pay heed to our feelings, our experiences, our own sense of things and our own inner voice and, out of that, to come to our own choices, decisions, conclusions and actions. We will respond in a protectively creative fashion when there are threats to being in touch with our own truth, when, for example, we are led to dishonour our own intuitions, when we are found wanting in our sense of things, when our feelings are dismissed as stupid or wrong. In such circumstances our creative efforts go into developing protective substitute strategies. We may, for example, attempt to become 'the best' at some endeavour such as sport, music, art or mathematics. Or, less obviously creatively, we may develop such substitute strategies as aggression or timidity. Or we may use illness as a substitute response in the face of threats to our creative self-expression.

There is a fundamental difference between open expression and protective expression of creativity. In creativity that arises from a place of safety, while it may be expressed in one particular aspect of human expression, such as music or interior design, the person will have a sense of self that does not equate with the particular expression of creativity. When creativity arises from repression and the protective behaviour of having to 'prove' self by being the best mathematician, best pianist, best athlete or best artist, a tremendous imbalance is present, producing great fear and pressure. The person who identifies self with his or her creative expression is highly vulnerable to the threat of losing the position of 'best'. Serious illness or suicide are possibilities in such tragic cases.

When other safeties – physical, sexual, emotional, intellectual, behavioural and social – are present, creative safety also tends to be present. Nonetheless, it is wise to ensure that the opportunities are provided for all individuals to live out their unique existence in an open, free and spontaneous way.

The Self's Response to Unsafety

Safety encapsulates the nature of the relationship that is required for expression of the self to be unhindered. Any blocks to the self's expression lead to either repression or suppression of that aspect of self that elicited threatening responses. Repression tends to be pre-verbal (before the development of speech) and occurs unconsciously, while suppression tends to be post-verbal (after the development of speech) and occurs consciously. Suppression is more common in adulthood, when we are less vulnerable than in childhood. However, most adult suppressions arise from earlier repressions. Both repression and suppression can be signalled through illness, though the illnesses associated with repression tend to be more chronic and enduring than those that embody suppression. Repression happens at an unconscious level because the level of pain experienced is too much consciously to bear and is a common defence in early childhood. Its equivalent in later childhood and adulthood is denial, a powerful creation that puts out of consciousness abuse experiences. Repression is the first line of unconscious defence against the threats to wholeness encountered. Subsequently, particularly when the threats continue, the defence of repression may be buttressed by additional defences, such as the controlling of others, approval-seeking, compliance and aggression.

When the giving and the receiving of unconditional love are not present, then repression of those deepest longings quickly occurs and powerful substitute ways are created in their stead. The creation of substitute behaviours in different domains of self-expression is described in the following chapter.

3 Illness is No Different from Other Substitute Behaviours Created by Self

The Wholeness of Human Experience

There is a long philosophical tradition of treating the body separately from the mind, a philosophy that up to modern times has had strong hold in the medical arena. However, contemporary and research point to the unity of human functioning. It is well known that emotional experiences, for example, have physical embodiments such as hormonal changes, blood pressure changes and muscular changes and, likewise, physical experiences, such as physical injury, have emotional accompaniments. In this book we recognize the wholeness of human experience and see that responsiveness to illness requires not just physical treatment but, very importantly, also calls out for a psychological response. The thesis of the book with regard to psychological responsiveness is that physical illness is best treated as being the same as the other kinds of substitute strategies that the self necessarily, and unconsciously, develops in circumstances of psychological threat. Illness can indeed be a very powerful substitute strategy. Illness, perhaps better than any other substitute creation, gains affection and love for the person who is suffering it, in circumstances where it is not possible to gain these in a real and spontaneous way; after all, it is a heart of stone that does not melt at the sight of sickness, whether in a child or an adult.

The purpose of this chapter is to describe the many ingenious ways by which the self protects wholeness and to demonstrate how illness can serve the same protective intentions as other substitute responses in the various domains of expression available to the self.

The Creative Purpose of Substitute Behaviours

As described in the previous chapter, safe holding around the different forms of self-expression, in the different worlds you inhabit, is the crucial context for open, conscious, real being in the world. When the self recognizes that it is dangerous – when there is an absence of unconditional love – to be consciously real, to be consciously expressive, to be consciously authentic, it wisely and ingeniously finds a substitute way of holding its place of love, of holding its wholeness. The intention of any substitute behaviour always is to express and safeguard your wholeness – albeit in a substitute, unconscious way.

The substitute means that the self wisely and creatively employs when you are living in an unsafe environment serve a four-fold purpose: to protect wholeness, to ward off further threats, to bring attention to existing threats, and to signal the underlying repressed expressions of self that need to be brought into the light. These substitute means encapsulate, often in a metaphorical way, exactly the expressions of your self that have had to be repressed.

The reasons for the creation of the substitute behaviours may lie in the past or in the present, but are connected essentially with the quality of relationships. At all times – whether in childhood or in adulthood – it is the quality of our relationships with others which determines the choice of the self to manifest itself in substitute or real ways. In this psychological context, the Buddhist practice of 'loving kindness' makes such wise and total sense, as does the Christian message of 'love others as you would yourself'. Psychologists have identified unconditional love as the deepest longing of each and every human being. When unconditional love is enduringly present, the self basks in its light and expresses itself fully – no need for subterfuge, or for substitute strategies.

The reasons necessitating the creation of substitute behaviours may lie with remote relationships, springing, for example, from harsh parental abandonment in childhood, or from physical, emotional, sexual, intellectual violations in childhood by significant adults –

grandparents, child-minders, teachers, aunts, uncles, neighbours – or indeed by siblings or peers. In childhood, the self will wisely have assessed the dangers of being consciously expressive of the fullness of our nature and will have found ways to offset, or at least minimize, further abandonment and violations. Threats may continue, and indeed are likely to continue, in our adult relationships, and as adults, unless we have encountered significant others in our lives who held us unconditionally and supported us to be real, we will continue to maintain the substitute protective behaviours that we developed as children. However, when we find safety to operate more from the place of love, we will begin consciously, though perhaps tentatively, to manifest our true selves. The self awaits and, indeed, seeks to create, such opportunities throughout our lives.

Reasons necessitating the creation of substitute behaviours in the present can also be traced to the quality of present relationships, these relationships often mirroring the remote relationships that led in the first instance to repression of aspects of self-expression. Where threats continue, the self continues to find substitute ways to safeguard wholeness.

Different Types of Substitute Behaviour

The substitute means that the self wisely creates when your real self-expression is met with conditional relating, or resistance, or denigration, or invalidation, or invisibility, together make up what may be described as a shadow world. Just as your self-expression takes different forms – physical, emotional, social, behavioural, intellectual, sexual, creative – so your substitute means of gaining love may involve any, or several, of these expressions; this reflecting the level of safety around any particular expression. For example, you may be safe enough to be open, spontaneous and real in your intellectual expression – for example, free to make mistakes, able to respond to failure as a step in learning, willing to ask questions – but in your social expression you may be using substitute means to gain visibility and love; substitute means such as compliance, over-pleasing, approval-seeking or being controlling, manipulation and aggression. Illness belongs to the shadow world like other substitute behaviours.

The interruptions to self-expression that necessitate the creation of substitute behaviours can occur in any one or more of the domains of expression available to us as human beings. The interruptions arise from the substitute responses of others, which in turn arose from the substitute responses of the significant others in their lives. It is for this reason that people's defensive creations can be traced back several generations within the one family. When individuals' expressions of self are interrupted – and clearly the intensity, frequency and endurance of such interruptions are important factors – they wisely and creatively develop their own substitute responses. We know intuitively the dangers of being real and so we create alternative ways of holding our place of love, our place of wholeness. Our defensive responses may mirror or be directly opposite to the substitute behaviours that we have accurately perceived as threats to our well-being. Within any one family, each child creates his or her own responses to the threats encountered. Furthermore, the substitute creation will be the one most apt for the specific aspect of self-expression that is under threat – sexual, physical, emotional, intellectual, social, behavioural or creative. Some individuals experience threats across all the domains of self-expression, while, for others, the blocks may occur in one or more domains. Whatever the individual's experience, the main purpose of the substitute response is to hold a sense of wholeness in an alternative way when real holding is not present.

Our varied substitute behaviours can be usefully categorized into four main groups: substance addiction, acting-out behaviours, acting-in behaviours and embodiments. A substance addiction is where the self uses a particular substance – such as food, alcohol, drugs, possessions, money – to fill the void arising from absence of unconditional holding. Some examples of acting-out substitute behaviours include hyperactivity, defiance, aggression, blaming, being controlling, being dominant, being destructive. Some examples of acting-in substitute behaviours include shyness, self-criticism, perfectionism, compliance, being over-responsible. In the physical domain, our 'bad health' embodiments are one, very strong, means by which the self demonstrates its necessary creation of a shadow world, these embodiments having the further powerful function of attempting to correct whatever repression of self-expression has occurred in earlier life and that continues in present life. Some examples of embodiments include migraine headaches, back pain, recurring infections, colitis, bed-wetting, heart disease and cancer.

A Story of a Physical Substitute Behaviour

Many individuals experience interruptions to their physical self-expression – for example, through comparisons, put-downs, criticism, judgement, sarcasm, violence. The substitute responses to such interruptions are as myriad as the interruptions themselves – for example, obesity, anorexia nervosa, physical withdrawal, having to look 'perfect', addiction to cosmetics, uncertainty about appearance, taking endless time to get ready for a social occasion.

The story of one man who spent many hours of his life in front of a mirror illustrates powerfully his substitute physical creation for 'not losing face'. His mother had constantly found fault with his physical appearance and his agonizing in front of the mirror in order to ensure that 'there was nothing out of place', and that he 'looked perfect' served to eliminate the possibility of further experiences of rejection. The extremes he went to – spending hours in front of the mirror, closely examining his face and then studying himself from every angle before daring to go outside his door – indicate the level of threat the man was experiencing about his physical expression. Recall that a substitute behaviour does not bring peace of mind – in fact one of its purposes is through discomfort to keep attention on the fact that there is some issue that needs to be resolved – but it does reduce or eliminate the threats that exist to one aspect of our self-expression. In seeking aid for his compulsive substitute behaviour, the man was helped to respond to its underlying message and to bring into the light the disharmony in his inner terrain that was being signalled. It was only by responding to the deeper issue – the need to recognize his own unique beauty, to recognize that his physical presence is here for his purposes and not for others' benefit – that the man slowly but surely began to let go of his compulsion.

However, his preoccupation with his looks severely and deeply affected his relationship with his wife and their three children. He was extremely possessive of his wife and would frequently accuse her of looking at, or wanting to be with, other men. Regrettably, she personalized his taunts of 'whore' and 'bitch', and other such labels, and her substitute response was to become depressed, to the extent of often needing hospitalization. Their daughter, like her father, became obsessed with her looks and both sons became addicted to alcohol, both also admitting to 'hating' their looks. It was a sad, sad instance of the 'sins of the father (projections) and the sins of the mother (introjection) being visited on the children'. The substitute responses of the children were every bit as creative and powerful as those of their parents. However, redemption – a return to being real and authentic – is possible for each member of a distressed family when one of the members seeks the appropriate professional help for his or her devastating entrapment in the shadow world.

A Story of an Emotional Substitute Behaviour

When it comes to emotional expression, the self exhibits an awesome array of responses, ranging from the depths of despair to the heights of ecstasy, from the quagmire of terror to the rock solidity of fearlessness. The dictionary contains hundreds of words indicating different emotions; it is crucial that we have the safety to express the full, rich range of the emotions available to us. We still live in cultures where emotions are suppressed, dismissed, disdained, ridiculed, considered 'wimpish', but the truth is that there is no clearer or more powerful window into our inner terrain than our emotions – our 'emergency' feelings alert us when something is wrong, when our well-being is at risk, while our 'welfare' feelings let us know when we are safe with no threat to well-being. The emergency feelings with which we tend to be most familiar are fear, sadness, depression, guilt, jealousy, envy, insecurity, vulnerability and grief. Some of the more familiar welfare feelings are joy, confidence, security, enthusiasm, hope, excitement, contentment. Emergency feelings arise in response to perceived threats to well-being but these feelings, such as depression and anxiety, can also be used by the self as a substitute means of calling attention to the suppression of broader emotional expression.

The story of a young man who presented with depression serves to illustrate the self's creation of depression as a substitute for genuine emotional spontaneity. This single man in his mid-thirties had, at the age of twenty-two, been diagnosed as suffering from endogenous depression by a psychiatrist and prescribed antidepressants. He had been advised that he would need medication for the rest of his life and that he would be unwise to attempt to forgo its use.

Clearly, the medication was not reducing his depression as, thirteen years later, he sought the help of one of the present authors following attendance at a public lecture. He had a secure career, but had difficulties maintaining relationships with women. In his current life, he allowed all his major life decisions to be made by his mother. His mother had always dominated him and could be violent when he showed any sign of individuality, spontaneity, independence or 'dare-devil' behaviour. As a child, in the face of the very threatening responses of his mother and the passivity of his father – who failed to champion his son's right to live his own life – he wisely suppressed all his feelings of anger, rage, hurt, fear, and suppressed his right to the expression of his own uniqueness and his right to live out his own life. He felt an overwhelming sense of 'feeling down' (depression), which metaphorically represented the continual substitute need to 'keep down' what was too dangerous to reveal. The depression was a substitute creation, in that it allowed him to talk about how 'down' he felt, without revealing the deeper truth of the situation, which would have been hugely perilous. In receiving attention for the depression and giving covert expression to his entrapped situation, he managed to find some degree of equilibrium.

The depression also cleverly pointed to serious repressions that had occurred in early childhood that were crying out for the necessary safety that would enable him to live his life in a real rather than a substitute manner. The psychotherapeutic relationship provided the unconditional love that was absent in the significant relationships in his life and, consequentially, in his relationship with himself. Over time, the presence of unconditional love provided him with the opportunity to take on the responsibility of being true to self and to live out his own, individual life spontaneously, with expression of the full range of emotions available to us as human beings.

A Story of an Intellectual Substitute Behaviour

It is in our nature to show natural curiosity, to have an eagerness to learn, to love to learn, and to do so in our own particular ways. Intelligence is a given, but its expression can be so chronically punished and criticized that it is no wonder the majority of people 'go for the average' – an extraordinarily clever means of reducing threats to intellectual expression – rather than manifesting their immense power. The confusion of knowledge with intelligence has been one of the great 'sins' of education, along with the rewarding of success and the punishment of failure. Success and failure are integral to learning and it has been a tragedy that what is intrinsic has been made extrinsic, resulting in the substitute perception of learning as a threat rather than the adventure it deserves to be.

The addiction to success – a great block to individual and societal progress – has become a common phenomenon. It arises in the early years of childhood and is reinforced in classrooms and work environments. The story of a medical student, who had been a high achiever all throughout her school life, serves to show the ingenious substitute behaviour she developed in order to reduce threats to her intellectual expression. Both her parents, through their own addiction to success and their high academic expectations, had put immense pressure on their daughter to be 'top of the class'. At age seven she put intense effort into being the best and would get extremely upset (a clever substitute response in itself) when she made a mistake or when a classmate outshone her. Her teachers reinforced her substitute responses, rather than identifying the risk inherent in her over-achievements. At age fifteen, prior to an important state school examination, she developed anorexia nervosa. Regrettably, she received only medical treatment for the condition, even though it was a clear cry for somebody to see how 'starved' she was of unconditional love.

She first came to the authors' attention when her mother rang for help for her daughter, whom she described as a third-year medical student who had taken to the bed and was refusing to talk to anybody. The young woman was complaining of being depressed and feeling suicidal and felt her life was over, following failure (her first experience of failure) at a particular oral examination. Suicide is always a possibility when the strongest substitute behaviour – in this case the young woman's addiction to success – fails in its attempt to ward off what is experienced as a highly threatening experience – in this case, not measuring up to her parents' expectations. When unconditional love is not present, but what is present instead is a substitute means of gaining recognition, a child will cleverly adopt the opportunity of the substitute means. In this case, success became the young woman's alternative way of 'being loved' by her parents but, sadly, the intense pressure to maintain their attention had continued from childhood right up to her current life as a young adult. An examination failure was the nightmare she had sought so hard to offset and now the 'evil day' had arrived. In response, the self now required further substitute responses – suicidal feelings, depression, insomnia, the recurrence of anorexia nervosa, and refusal to talk (how powerful was this last response, since it prevented the possibility of the truth being revealed).

The addiction to success is such a clever creation: firstly, because success becomes the new means of being seen (the presence of her unique self had not gained her unconditional love); secondly, it signals the repression of the true self that needs to be released; and thirdly, it points to the nature of the relationship that is needed for a return to harmony, that is a relationship of unconditional love. Initially, the young woman was very reluctant to receive help and to be open to an unconditional relationship. This reluctance made total sense, because it was a protection against becoming real, which would mean going against the parental conditions for recognition – a terrifying prospect. With her permission, the parents were invited to come for psychotherapy and gradually they became open to looking at their own stories and the impact that their substitute responses had had on their daughter. As relationships between them shifted from conditional to unconditional, the young woman began to re-find the adventure of learning and, most importantly, came to the realization that she 'was not an examination result'.

A Story of a Behavioural Substitute Response

Every adult and child needs to shout from the rooftops 'I am not my behaviour'. The confusion of self with behaviour removes the essence of what relationship is all about – unconditional love. Love needs to stand separately from any behaviour or personal quality. But the sad reality is that we are most often judged for our behaviour and are often labelled educationally, medically, psychiatrically or psychologically. Behaviour is a creation of the self; it arises either from a place of unconditional love or from fear. Whatever arises is necessary and always has an intention. When behaviour emerges from a place of unconditional love, it is, for example, kind, supportive, non-judgemental, non-possessive, encouraging, genuine, empowering and definite. When behaviour arises from a place of fear, it can, for example, be aggressive, passive, timid, manipulative, controlling, indecisive, arrogant, acquiescent, violent, perfectionist and obsessive. What is important to see is that each of the examples of behaviour arising from fear are substitute responses that are created in the face of blocks to genuine behavioural expression. Any difficult behaviour, whether from child or adult, is enacted, not to make life difficult for another, but to demonstrate how difficult life is for the person exhibiting the substitute behaviour.

Exaggerated politeness is one substitute response that may arise from a child trying to counter 'never getting it right' for a parent who is hypercritical and, no matter how much one tries, always harshly highlights the one thing that was not done. The child in this case is so terrified of re-experiencing the rejecting response from the parent that the child will 'bend over backwards' to please. And when there is even a hint that the child may have been the source of displeasure, the child will go to extremes to end any possible upset that he or she fears he or she may have caused.

Such creative responses were exhibited in the case of a married woman in her thirties, who presented with a terrible dread of upsetting people. She would agonize for days or weeks about an encounter with her mother, or sister, or brother, or friend, where she felt she might have upset the other person. In her childhood her mother – who engaged heavily in the substitute behaviour of 'wanting everything right' and waiting hand and foot on everybody but herself and her daughter – enslaved her daughter to her perfectionism. Her daughter, in turn, created her own counter substitute behaviours of perfectionism, along with an over-eagerness to please, exaggerated politeness and a constant seeking of reassurance that she had not inflicted any hurt on the other. These are wonderful and very strong substitutes in the face of the tide of rejection responses she experienced as a child and continued to be in dread of as an adult.

Each one of the young woman's substitute behaviours has the intention of eliminating any possibility of getting it wrong and exposing herself to criticism and rejection. The substitute responses never fully resolve the threat to well-being – only unconditional love can do that – but they do powerfully reduce the frequency and intensity of the threat. In reducing the threats, the substitute behaviours serve the purpose for her of holding, albeit temporarily, a sense of her wholeness. These defensive responses further served to highlight the major repressions of her sense of lovability, her spontaneity, her right to make mistakes, her right to live her own life and be separate and independent of her mother – powerful repressions requiring powerful substitute responses. The recovery of self and the fullness of spontaneous behavioural expression, for which her substitute behaviours were loudly calling, has been a slow process but an increasingly freeing experience for this young woman. When you have been harshly and frequently unloved in your early years and this experience endures into adulthood, it can be terrifying to take the risk again to reach out for unconditional love.

A Story of a Social Substitute Behaviour

There is a very wise need in us as human beings to belong. We want to belong to a partner, to a family, a group, a community, a workplace, a church. This belonging creates the solid ground for the deeper need to belong to ourselves. These two needs are inter-related. Ultimately, it is the responsibility of each adult to belong to self and from that inner stronghold of self to acknowledge and value the presence of each other person we encounter. Relationship lies at the heart of human well-being, but many individuals are hurt, disappointed, even devastated, at encountering an over-belonging or an under-belonging or a no-belonging in their lives. For example, many individuals in the workplace complain of anonymity and many students complain of not being valued in the classroom. It is each person's presence and absence that needs to matter within any social system.

An over-belonging is where your belonging, for example to your mother, involves your allowing her to live her life through you; you are not seen for yourself but for being helpless and dependent. An under-belonging is where you are valued not for your unique presence but for a specific behavioural contribution – for example, being clever, being a 'worker', being 'good', being athletic, being accomplished. Your response in this case may be to become addicted to producing the condition for belonging and, now, the door to expression of your unique presence has been solidly closed. Only when safety to be self in a social context is created in the future will you be able to redeem your true self from the realm of repression. The following story illustrates how social expression can become so severely blocked.

This young woman, in her early twenties, had recently arrived at university to study psychology. In regard to her intellectual self-expression, she had had safe holding in her early years and, accordingly, felt secure about her ability to do the course, and to understand and take in its intellectual content. But she was not similarly secure in regard to her social self-expression. The young woman grew up in a rural area, in a family that kept to itself, to parents who had a certain status in the local community because both were professionals – in other words, two people who were considered to be 'smart', educated, and of 'superior' standing relative to other members of the community. As a child, she took on this aura of 'superiority'; this being a powerful cover-up for the insecurity that was present in both her parents and that was preventing them from providing safe holding for her around social expression. In her school-going years, this substitute behaviour had succeeded in warding off the threat of being 'found wanting', and her 'superiority' had never been challenged.

However, when she arrived at university, she was now exposed to peers who were not taking on the role of 'inferior' status to her 'superior' status, peers who were confident in their own different views, perceptions, experiences of life and whom she found very challenging. When her old substitute strategy no longer worked, she was now under threat and found herself becoming very anxious about speaking in class, and uneasy about having any attention directed towards her. Her protective substitute behaviours manifested as shyness, a low, weak, hesitant voice, reticence and trembling hands. Her anxious substitute behaviours served the purpose of avoiding being seen and, thus, warding off the threat of possible rejection and the humiliation of being found 'inferior'. The anxiety, in its discomfort for the young woman, served the further purpose of drawing her attention to her felt unsafety in her current environment. The deeper purpose of the anxiety was to bring into conscious awareness the unsafe holding in her earlier life around social self-expression; this unsafety arising from the conditional – based on comparisons with others in the local community – sense of her social self. A further element of the unsafe holding came from a mother who herself was anxious in social situations, hidden under a veneer of reserve. The ultimate resolution needed for the young woman was for her to find her unconditional sense of her social self; to know herself to be one of a kind and special, unique, incomparable to any other and without need to compare.

A Story of a Sexual Substitute Behaviour

Considerable pleasure and fulfilment can be experienced in human sexual expression. Yet it is one of the expressions of self that has suffered, and continues to suffer greatly from a fear of, and condemnation of, sexuality in religious proscriptions, social taboo and commercial exploitation. There is the added, very serious, factor of the sexual violation of children. Whatever the sources of threat to authentic sexual self-expression, these threats are transported through relationship. Much of adult sexual immaturity is a substitute response to the threats to sexual expression experienced in childhood, in relationships with adults, siblings or peers, within homes, classrooms, communities, churches and recreational facilities. A common substitute sexual behaviour among men is performance anxiety. The following story illustrates the creative wisdom in this kind of substitute behaviour.

A young single man in his mid-twenties presented with major anxiety about his sexual potency. There were two aspects to his anxiety: one was concerned with premature ejaculation during intercourse with his girlfriend; the other concerned a fear of losing his erection during foreplay. He also feared not satisfying his partner. When a man associates his sense of self with an erection – and in Western culture this is quite a common association – his anxiety has the substitute purpose of ensuring that he does all in his power to hold his erection, by employing fantasy, eroticism, pornography. He is not yet in a place to say to his partner: 'I am not my erection.' Indeed, the man needs to go much further than that and assert: 'I have sexual potency, feelings and needs but I am not any of those things.' It is remarkable that when men achieve separateness from each of their expressions of self – physical, sexual, emotional, intellectual, behavioural, social and creative – that is the time when they are at their most powerful, comfortable with having an erection, losing an erection, having no erection. They are also comfortable with premature ejaculation and can accept that, with experience, they can learn to have more charge over ejaculation. They can have a greater sensitivity to the fact that sex is about mutual pleasuring and sexuality is about intimacy, about one unique human being intimately meeting another unique human being.

The sources of this young man's creative anxieties were: lack of sexual education, the subject of sexuality being considered a 'taboo' subject at home, and sexuality being treated as a means to an end among his peers, and in the wider culture. He was greatly relieved to find the unconditional support to realize that 'he is not his erection' and to discover, through sexual education, that premature ejaculation – due to heightened arousal – is a common experience among young men. He began to realize that he was not the freak he thought himself to be. His anxiety served to ensure that he would do his utmost to maintain an erection, and it served the further important purpose of avoiding the possibility of rejection, but crucially it pointed to the deeper issue that needed to be resolved – the identification of self with a sexual behaviour.

A Story of a Creative Substitute Behaviour

Creativity has become so identified with art, literature, fashion, architecture and music there is an assumption that unless you are accomplished in one of these fields you are not creative! Creativity is part and parcel of our nature; it is not determined by its expressions. Something that is often missed – and a serious omission it is – is that each child within a family fashions his or her own particular responses to the family dynamics. Furthermore, each child finds his or her own particular way of being in the world and creates a repertoire of personal qualities and behaviours that very definitely mark off him or her from siblings. It is the wise parent and teacher who build on these creative expressions of individuality. Treating all children as if they were the same is one of the great 'sins' of parenting and teaching.

However, it is essential that the self of the child, or the adult, is not confused with his or her creativity. The self is, indeed, marvellously creative, but the self is not its creativity. Many individuals learn to identify themselves with their creative expressions and can suffer greatly when these do not receive the looked-for acclaim from others.

The following story of a journalist brings home the tragedy of confusing self with one's particular creative expression. This individual frequently talked in therapy about what 'a great piece' he had written for his newspaper. He would be as 'high as a kite' about the accomplishment. When asked about what would happen should the day come when he did not write a great piece, his response was alarming: 'No, no, that will never happen. I'll make sure I keep up to my high standard. I couldn't take it if I fell short.' The source of his addiction to being the best and the fears of falling off the pedestal was his father's unrealistic expectation that 'nothing less than being top of his class' would satisfy him. As a result of the pressure to live up to this condition for recognition from his father, he applied himself tooth and nail to his school work, particularly to writing, as he had won several prizes for his essay writing. These prizes pleased his father no end; the sad reality being that the father failed to see the real prize (gift) of his son's presence. Considerable work was needed to guide this man towards doing what his father had failed to do – to find unconditional acceptance of self and to reclaim the adventure of learning, of creativity, and of work.

Illness as a Creative Substitute Response

It may seem like a paradox but illness, while a threat to our physical well-being, has the same psychological healing purpose as any substitute creations in any of the other domains of expression available to the self. The strange truth is that it takes an illness at one level to heal an even greater illness at another level. The psycho-social illness of inner disharmony and a lack of consciousness of how our inner terrain, moment by moment, determines our every word and action can lead to serious illness. Such a psycho-social state is the greatest threat, not only to the individual but to the world of people and nature – 'What doth it profit a man should he gain the whole world, but suffer the loss of his soul?' (Matthew 16:26). As outlined in the stories above, the purpose of any substitute behaviour is not to harm us, but to bring to attention in an indirect way the care that is needed but is not safe for us to seek in a conscious way. The embodiment of the unconscious repression of some expression of self is wisely designed to try to ensure that wholeness, the place of unconditional love, is maintained. The greater the disharmony in your inner terrain, the more serious the illness created may need to be, particularly if you are not yet safe enough in your world to respond to the meaning and purpose of the symptoms. Sadly, the most common response to physical illness is that it is a nuisance, an embarrassment, something that should not happen and something that always comes at the wrong time. There are few of us who embrace illness for what it is – a wise creation of the self that is attempting to bring to the surface what has been necessarily hidden but, as a result, has been left in the shadow world of abandonment. When the illness is of a serious nature, an individual may respond to it with denial, fear, rage, promises to God and others that 'I'll change my ways'. The last response is so close to what the self, through the serious illness, is attempting to do but, because it is coming from a place of fear rather than love and understanding, the changes brought about may be surface ones and not last very long.

A Story of Illness as a Substitute Response

The following story of a teenager who presented with long-standing, secondary enuresis – involuntary urination – illustrates the wise process of the manifestation of unconscious repression of an aspect of self-expression through physical embodiment. This teenager had been bed-wetting every night for fourteen years and by the time he came for help, the enuresis had become a serious source of embarrassment for him. He dreaded that his peers would discover his problem and he was highly motivated to 'be cured'. He had undergone several medical interventions over the years, but the prescribed medications did nothing to alter the problem. He had also attended a behavioural psychologist, who had prescribed a bed-alarm but he effectively slept through the alarm. He was somewhat surprised when the therapist suggested that they would work together to dis-cover how the bed-wetting had helped him over the past fourteen years. The focus of the therapeutic process was to uncover the inten-tions of this long-standing embodiment; particularly to explore what the bed-wetting currently stopped him from doing, what it made him do, and what hidden disharmony was being signalled.

He remembered that the bed-wetting started when he was around three years of age. As other memories began to surface, he recounted being very frightened, distressed and enraged by his father's coming home drunk every night, shouting and being violent towards his mother and older brother and sister. This situation had not changed over the years and his mother continued to be passive and trauma-tized in the face of her husband's dark behaviours. When asked how he had managed all this turmoil and whether or not he had had anybody to whom he could confide his experiences, he told of how he could not go to his mother because he was afraid of upsetting her more than she already was; he was terrified his mother would 'fall apart' were he to express his feelings. This was a wise protector – he could not risk losing his mother, because, even in her passivity, she represented the only security he had. In response to the query of what happened to all those powerful feelings he dared not express, he shrugged saying: 'I don't know. Buried them, I suppose.'

In the safety of the unconditional therapeutic relationship, he began to see how he was expressing his feelings through his bladder; metaphorically he was 'blathering' about his trauma through his bed-wetting. He understood that if he had not found a substitute way to express what was going on in his life, he would have exploded. The embodiment helped him to stop holding in his feel-ings and to express them in some way by releasing his bladder. The opportunity was now there for him to do consciously what he had been doing unconsciously through his body; this was the challenge and the resolution for him. Up to this time he had not even remotely connected the enuresis with the family conflicts; this being yet another repression of consciousness that was necessary until he found a safe relationship that would provide the security and the loving holding that would empower him to make the connection.

Gradually, this teenager began to express consciously what he felt, not just about the past but also about the present: first with the therapist; then, with the championing of the therapist, a good friend; then with a relative; and finally he spoke with his mother and with his father. The bed-wetting actually stopped quite quickly; it had served its purpose and done so very well; once its meaning and intention were responded to with acknowledgement and care, and with commitment to restoring the safe emotional environment that he had always deserved but so sadly lacked.

In approaching this teenager's enuresis as a wise creation of the self in an unsafe environment, the following points are highlighted:

- The enuresis was there not to make life difficult for the youth himself or for others; it was an ingenious creation to bring attention to how difficult life was for him since his early childhood.
- The embodiment served the purpose of doing in a substitute way what was not safe to do openly and consciously – to release his feelings.
- The enuresis stopped the youth from 'holding on' to his feelings.
- The location of the embodiment – the bladder – metaphorically made a lot of sense to the youth. In Ireland, the term to 'blather on' is commonly used to refer to 'going on and on' about a subject. The metaphors used by the individual are gleaned from the particular local or national culture and need to be interpreted in that context.
- Exploration of the metaphors in the language used by the youth brought further understanding of why this particular embodiment had been created: he spoke of 'being pissed off' with his father; of his father 'getting pissed'; of fear of 'turning on the water works' in regard to his mother.
- The embodiment threw clear light on the troubles within the family.

- Most of all, the embodiment helped the youth to realize the responsibility for the conscious expression of how he felt and to express his unmet needs in his family relationships.
- Emotional and social safety were the critical contexts to enable the youth to realize what he consciously had to do in order that the substitute response in the form of the enuresis was no longer required.
- The attention attracted by the embodiment also provided the opportunity for the other family members consciously to recognize the lack of unconditional loving in the family.

Providing a Compassionate Response to Illness

The compassionate response being called out for by illness is the same as that for any other substitute behaviour created by the self:

- Acknowledgement of its creative purpose
    - to do in a substitute way what is not safe to do in a direct, conscious way;
    - to alert us to the repressions unconsciously resorted to in order to survive the dark behaviours of others;
    - to alert us to the fundamental need to return to the place of unconditional love.
- Provision of the safety – unconditional relating – to explore the creative purposes of the illness.
- Provision of the safety of loving kindness to explore what could now be done differently; how the underlying disharmony in the person's inner terrain might be resolved openly, directly and consciously.
- Provision of support, encouragement, guidance to allow the person to experiment with the open, conscious care of self.

4 Causes and Intentions of Illness:
Separate but Equal Concerns

Searching for Causes; Searching for Intentions

The causes of illness are the preoccupation of general medical science and also of psychosomatic medicine. The focus of this book is not on the causes of illness but on an equally important dimension of illness – its psychological intentions. While causes are not the focus here, psychosomatic medicine, with its recognition of the involvement of psycho-social factors in illness, nevertheless forms an important bridge between the physical emphasis in medicine and the psychological emphasis in this book.

In medical science, exploration of causes has enabled the tracing of particular illnesses to certain purely physical factors such as viruses, bacteria, genetic defects, infections, organ damage, failure of the immune system and physical injury. But even in medical science the link between physically based factors and illnesses is not straight-forward. Studies have shown, for example, that where a virus exists within a closed community, only a small number of the community develop the symptoms of the virus-caused disease. A similar phenomenon was observed in the situation where bacteria had been administered in error to a group of people and only a small number of that group went on to develop the bacteria-caused disease.

Psychosomatic medicine broadens the exploration of causes by positing that certain illnesses can be traced to psycho-social factors involving the person's developmental, learning, emotional and social life experiences. Medical science does not deny the reality of psycho-social links to the onset, endurance, therapeutic response to and outcome of a given illness. Nor does psychosomatic medicine deny that some illnesses are a direct result of some physically based factor. We also accept that certain illnesses have physical sources and others have psycho-social rather than physical causes, but in this book we are concerned with the intentions of all illnesses, whether their sources involve physical or psycho-social factors.

Within the discipline of psychosomatic medicine there is a specific set of illnesses for which there appears to be no dispute regarding their psychological origins; these being referred to as psycho-physiological illnesses. In regard to psycho-physiological illnesses, it is now accepted that if the psychological factors are not resolved, the illness will worsen or recur. The belief is that when a person is chronically and frequently emotionally distressed, intense physiological responses are likely to follow and, unless resolved, may become life-threatening. [See p. 65] The more common psycho-physiological conditions are:

- high blood pressure/low blood pressure
- migraine headaches
- hyperventilation and asthma
- peptic ulcers
- anorexia nervosa
- menstrual disturbances
- sexual impotence/frigidity
- frequent urination.

Certain characteristics have been found to be common to these illnesses:

- The conditions involve organs of the autonomic nervous system.
- The conditions are typically accompanied by a high anxiety state.
- The psycho-physiological responses appear to result from a prolonged effect of natural reactions to emotional stress.
- The psycho-physiological responses are likely to result in physical illnesses that can be life-threatening.

In the literature on stress there are many examples of a link between psycho-social factors and the onset of illness, the most frequently noted link being that between the body's 'fight or flight' response to perceived threats in one's psycho-social environment. When there are prolonged physiological responses to enduring physical or emotional threats that are not being resolved, then excessive secretion of corticosteroids can lead to such diseases as ulcers, hypertension and heart disease. The stress literature speaks of threats to well-being in terms of external and internal stressors; the more common stressors associated with onset of disease being:

- death of a spouse
- death of a parent before the age of sixteen
- school and university examinations
- loss of an important relationship
- serious illness of a parent
- advent of a sibling as a rival
- desertion by a parent or a spouse
- loss of paid employment
- bullying
- perfectionism
- addiction to success
- being a workaholic.

The kinds of disease that have been found to arise following such stressors are: heart disease, cancer, leukaemia, hyperthyroidism, pulmonary tuberculosis, pernicious anaemia, multiple sclerosis, ulcerative colitis, Raynaud's disease and asthma. Of course, not everybody responds to stressful life events with serious illness; bearing out the point of this book that a crucial factor in the onset of illness is the nature of the individual's inner terrain and consequent creative responses to stressful life experiences. In the situation where a serious illness follows a major loss, the illness can disappear on the re-establishment of the relationship with the lost person (or a substitute) and reappear if there is a second separation or the threat of separation. Furthermore, if the medical doctor is perceived as the substitute replacement for the lost person, any threat of discharge can lead to a recurrence of the life-threatening illness, and the reinstatement of the relationship leads to the disappearance of the medical condition. If this situation were to be explored from the point of view of the intentions of the self, a reasonable hypothesis would be that the person has developed the substitute response of dependence on relationship with another, in the face of early threats to social self-expression, and is trying to bring forward, through the process of the illness, the disharmony in his or her inner terrain and his or her need to develop self-reliance.

Further to positing that psycho-social factors are the cause of certain illnesses, psychosomatic medicine holds that all illnesses, whatever their origin, are affected by the psycho-social responses of the person who is ill. For example, it has been found that when a person develops a depressive response to a diagnosis, say of cancer, the prognosis can be adversely affected. Bernie Siegel (Siegel, 1986), in his work as an oncologist, discovered what he called 'exceptional' individuals – those who were given a poor prognosis, but who just wanted to 'get on with their lives' – either totally recovered or lived longer than had been medically expected. However, for those persons who, following diagnosis, 'threw in the towel', even though the prognosis was good, the progress of their illness was accelerated beyond medical expectations. One of the main goals of psychosomatic medicine is to identify those psycho-social responses that increase susceptibility to illness, as well as those that enhance resistance to and an adaptive coping with illness.

Richard Totman (Totman, 1982), in *The Social Causes of Illness*, comes to several conclusions that resonate with the focus of our book on the psychological intentions of illness:

- The individual must be the fundamental unit in examining why disease occurs.
- There needs to be a way of examining the *meaning* of illness with the individuals afflicted. Totman recommends that the focus of the examination must be 'the world of actions, purposes and intentions and the mechanisms underlying an individual's understanding of his world'.
- There is 'an embarrassment of riches' in the links between psycho-social events and physiological responses.

The Need for the Search for Intentions

Alongside the search for causes, there is another very powerful search that needs to be undertaken – the search for the intention, purpose or meaning of the illness. There is intelligence to all human behaviour – physical, emotional, social, sexual, intellectual and creative. If we bear this intelligence in mind, then it can be seen that while causes may be general – for example, a particular virus may be the cause of the occurrence of a particular illness in many people – the intention of the illness will be peculiar to each individual afflicted. The discovery of the virus as the cause of the illness provides a powerful guide to the physical treatment required, but a comprehensive, compassionate response to the person who is ill requires understanding of the meaning and intention of the illness in the context of the person's unique life story and life circumstances.

In finding a truly compassionate response to illness, the challenge is to 'pull out all the stops' and, alongside the physical treatment arising from the understanding of the illness's physical or psycho-social causes, to put in place the psycho-social responses that are appropriate to an understanding of the psycho-social intentions underlying the illness. This kind of all-out response is not an easy challenge; many people – especially adult males – might be described as 'emotionally illiterate'; this arising from threats to emotional self-expression in relationships – especially in childhood, but also in current relationships. Accordingly, not only the persons experiencing illness, but also those involved in any way in their care, need guidance and safe holding to enable the underlying intentions of the illness to be uncovered.

The medical science literature shows clearly how complex the search for causes is, and how, alongside excitement and breakthrough, the search is fraught with setbacks, reversals, highs and lows of optimism, and changes of direction with ever-growing new information and research. The search for intention and meaning is no less complex, exciting and fraught but, sadly, has not attracted the same level of dedication, persistence and application of intelligence and creativity. Our understanding of the place of illness in human life, and our ability to respond to illness compassionately and comprehensively, would be greatly enhanced if the focus on the person's external world were to be accompanied by an equal focus on the person's interior world. The heart of well-being, of wholeness, is love, and relationship is the medium of love; these are experiences that belong in one's inner world.

Love: The Heart of Wholeness

Since love is the heart of wholeness, a full understanding of the meaning and intention of illness requires exploration of the nature of relationships within and between people in our different social systems – family, school, community, workplace, church, society. Illness calls out for attention to how we are relating to ourselves in the first place and, out of that, how we are relating to others. Illness is an ingenious and powerful means of drawing attention to the central issue of human life – love – because even the most 'hardhearted' tend to be 'softened' around illness. Illness then has psycho-social intentions: to harmonize the relationship with ourselves (psychological issue) and to harmonize the relationship with others (sociological issue).

The Need to Create Safe Social Systems

Just as there exists strong commitment to research on the causes of illness, there needs equally to be research on how the social systems of which we are part operate to hinder or create the safety individuals need to be fully expressive of their true loving nature, because it is this safety that determines whether or not we have to create substitute behaviours such as illness.

The family, the school and the workplace are three key social systems within which the nature of the relationships we experience has very significant implications for whether or not we find ourselves having to create the substitute behaviour of illness.

The Need for Safe Family Relationships

It is well established that certain illnesses run in families as a result of some common physical cause such as a genetic defect. What is not so obvious, but also true, is that the repression of loving relationships may express itself in similar illness embodiments among family members and across the generations of a family. In an emotionally unsafe family environment, it is clever to adopt a defence strategy that is similar to that of one's parents; the old saying 'if you can't beat them, join them' – the defence mechanism of identification – makes psychological sense. There are many accounts of the operation of the defence mechanism of identification in situations of great emotional, sexual or physical threat. Survivors of wartime concentration camps provide many stark examples of their experiences at the hands of other prisoners who identified with their captors. It is a terrible tragedy, but true, that some families can also be highly threatening to children's welfare and some marriages to the partners' welfare. If parents carry their repressions into the creation of a family, it is inevitable that children will suffer and a cycle of embodiments of those repressions will begin.

Most family doctors are aware that children's recurring infections, aches and pains, enuresis, soiling and asthma are psycho-social in origin, but we need to explore more deeply the connections between the embodiments exhibited by children and their relationship experiences within the family and, beyond the family, in the school and community. It may turn out to be that the most powerful way of preventing illness is to empower adults to come into their own wholeness, so that when they come to be parents, they do not bring into the relationships with their children their own repressions and consequent emotional vulnerabilities. There is now much accumulated knowledge on what is needed to create healthy families and marriages – physically, sexually, emotionally, intellectually and socially. But what is not so well recognized is the need for relationship training for parenthood, and indeed for marriage, relationship training that is focused on the individuals involved becoming self-possessed, so that they, in turn, can create empowering relationships with others where there are less of the kinds of threat that necessitate the creation of substitute behaviours such as illness.

The Need for Safe School Relationships

School is a highly significant 'world' for young people and the nature of the holding they experience in the relationships in this world has important consequences for whether they are more in shadow or in openness in their inner terrain. While over the last decades there has been a growing recognition in the school world of physical needs related to exercise, healthy eating and sexual activity, the quality of relationships in the school social system has hardly been considered. The effects of bullying on children, and the frequent embodiment of the repressions that are the result of it, are well known to psychologists, psychiatrists and general practitioners; the most common embodiments being abdominal pain, vomiting, frequent infections, skin problems, headaches, enuresis and encopresis (involuntary defecation). Some further common substitute behaviours created in the face of bullying include depression, anxiety, self-harming, para-suicide, and suicide. Clearly, the relationships between the students themselves need to be guided towards openness and kindness but, equally, the relationships between teachers and students, and teachers and teachers, require serious consideration. Teachers deserve opportunities to explore their own inner terrains and to discover how to create safe relationships with students and with colleagues. It is of note that research on stress has shown teaching to be a high health-risk profession.

The Need for Safe Work Relationships

There is research to suggest that 60 per cent of lost work time is due to absenteeism resulting from lower back pain. A whole industry of therapies has developed for the treatment of back pain, including orthodox and what are sometimes referred to as 'alternative' therapies. Typically, the focus is on treating the physical symptoms; rarely are the psycho-social questions asked. Workplaces can be emotionally and socially dangerous places in which to be:

bullying is commonplace, undue pressures to perform are very frequent and the policy of profits before people is often practised. Despite this, few connect high absenteeism and employees' illnesses – whether psychosomatic or physical in origin – with the threats experienced in the work world. Sadly, as in the case of parents and teachers, leaders and managers in workplaces are not yet required to reflect on their level of self-reliance before taking on their particular roles. But there is a growing awareness of the importance of relationships within the workplace and a growing recognition that a positive work ethos reduces absenteeism and the prevalence of work-related illnesses, and, furthermore, increases productivity. As for the leaders of families and schools, leaders in the workplace need to be provided with the opportunities that will enable them to develop the kind of relationships that act as a prevention against the necessity of members of the work social system having to create substitute behaviours such as illness.

The Metaphorical Nature of Illness

In previous chapters you will have seen that unconditional love is the lifeblood of the self. The self always knows whether or not it is being held with unconditional love in its different expressions, and if there are threats to its wholeness, the self will find substitute ways of bringing the resultant disharmony in the inner terrain into the open. There is a myriad of substitute responses that the self can create, illness being one such powerful substitute. All substitute behaviours, of their very nature – below consciousness – operate through metaphors; metaphors that encapsulate precisely and aptly the hidden issues that need to be brought forward into consciousness. Illness operates in the same metaphorical way; there is metaphorical meaning in the nature of the illness itself, in its location in the body, and in the language used to describe its symptoms and accompanying physical experiences (see next chapter). But it is not always easy to read the metaphorical language of illness, and uncovering the self's intentions in creating the illness, is a subtle, sensitive, and sometimes painstaking process (see Chapters 6, 7 and 8).

In general terms, the intentions of any given illness are, as with any other substitute behaviour: to reduce the threats to well-being; to somehow draw attention to the threats that are present in the person's world; to alert us to the repressions of self-expression that, as a result of the threats, have had to occur at an unconscious level; and to bring into the open what needs to happen in order for the threats to be resolved and wholeness restored in a real way. Of course, in any one instance of illness, the illness symptoms will have unique intentions for the individual experiencing the embodiment. Back pain has already been mentioned as an example of a common embodiment. This condition can have a variety of metaphorical associations:

- 'I feel my back is against the wall.'
- 'He is getting my back up.'
- 'I am backing out of that.'
- 'I have no back-up.'
- 'I've too much on my back.'
- 'There are issues back there that I'm avoiding.'
- 'I feel like I have been stabbed in the back.'

It is for each person who experiences back pain to explore the possible metaphorical meanings it may have and to try to uncover what particular repression is being signalled by the embodiment. One of the present authors used to experience severe back pain and makes sense of it as follows:

The intentions of my lower back pain were, one, to alert me to my substitute response of an over-caring of others; two, to help bring this defensive response into consciousness; and, three, to move towards the real response of openly caring for and nurturing myself in a way that, up to then, had been too threatening for me to do consciously.

Initially, the episodes of back pain were effective in stopping the over-working, but the recurrence of the symptoms was a challenge to continue querying the condition, finally leading to the conscious realization of two underlying repressions that required resolution. The first repression was the sense that 'I *should* always be there for others', and the second was that 'I *should not* have any needs myself'. Metaphorically, the back pain symbolized taking too much on my back, backing out of nurturing myself, and getting my back up when blocked from acting out my creative compulsion to care for others.

The conscious realization that I needed to care openly for myself, to allow and support others to care for themselves, and to be tolerant in the face of difference, has led to non-recurrence of crippling back pain. I occasionally get a twinge but I can now quickly pay heed to the underlying intention and consciously set about correcting some neglect of myself that has begun to emerge.

It is in uncovering the intentions of an embodiment that we begin to see the wisdom and compassion of the self in illness. The intention is always concerned with maintenance of wholeness in a substitute way, until such time as we become safe enough to take conscious responsibility for the repressions that have had to occur. The ultimate healing of illness is psycho-social in nature, whereby the person takes responsibility for his or her own well-being, for his or her relationships with others, and for open, real expression of self.

Clues in Uncovering the Intentions of Illness

In going through the process of uncovering the intentions of a particular embodiment (see Chapter 6), the *location* of the illness, the *intensity* of the symptoms, its *frequency* and its *endurance* in present time and over time are important sources of information. Further significant sources of information are *life circumstances* at the time of onset, the actual *time of onset* itself, what is *currently happening internally* (thoughts, images, dreams, memories) and *externally* (work, relationships, responsibilities). How individuals describe their particular illnesses is central to understanding the intentions of the embodiments. Language often carries several meanings and it is wise to look at what is being said, not just literally but also metaphorically (see next chapter). In our experience, people's language about their physical symptoms can provide important clues to the underlying psycho-social problems that need urgent attention. For example, people say things such as 'My energy constantly lets me down'; 'My stomach can't hold food any more'; 'My back feels like it's breaking'; 'My chest aches'; 'My bowel is running away with itself'; 'My head is bursting'; 'I'm burning up with fever'.

In attempts to uncover the intentions of illness, and find the most comprehensively loving response to it, it is wise also to pay attention to what the body needs in terms of physical healing and the possibility that this may represent analogically what the self is calling to be done consciously. For example, the need for open heart surgery may be calling for a conscious opening up of the heart to self and others; the need to dissolve a blood clot may represent the conscious need to unblock a particular emotion, say, grief or anger. Observation, too, of what the illness forces you to stop doing and what it impels you to do can reveal much of the intentions of the self in the embodiment. For example, a man addicted to work catches a flu virus that, on the one hand, compels him to take a break from his work and, on the other hand, pushes him to rest and nurture himself – an activity that under normal circumstances he does not permit himself to do.

5 Location and Language of Illness:
Metaphorical Meanings

Aids to Uncovering the Intentions of Illness

In previous chapters you will have seen how ingenious the self is in using all the resources available to it – physical, sexual, emotional, social, intellectual, behavioural, creative – in order to create the kind of substitute responses that will most accurately and aptly represent, in a metaphorical manner, the hidden disharmonies in the inner terrain that need to be brought forward into consciousness. The physical embodiment of illness is one such substitute creation that carries powerful metaphorical meanings, signposting what is amiss and the resolutions needed.

As described in Chapter 4, apart from whatever may be the physical cause of an illness, it has underlying psychological meaning and intention. Our aim in this chapter is to show how everyday language involving the body part affected by the particular illness, and the physical function of the body part in question, can provide very powerful clues in the process of uncovering the intentions of the self in creating whatever substitute embodiment may be present. The self is always concerned with safeguarding wholeness and will creatively use whatever means are available to it to signal the presence of threats to any aspect of self-expression.

The layered meanings of the language we use in our everyday lives constitute one powerful resource that the self uses to convey metaphorically what is not safe to convey openly and consciously. It can be useful to look at words in ways other than their literal meaning. For example, we can see that 'earth' is an anagram for 'heart' – this seems meaningful, since as humans we tend to see the earth as the heart of the universe and we see ourselves as being at the heart of creation. Another example is 'information' – a word in frequent usage in these times – which can be broken down as 'in-formation', pointing to the fact that unless knowledge informs our living, it serves little or no purpose. Similarly, the word 'confusion' can be broken down into 'con' (against) and 'fusion' (union with self), and 'conform' can be broken down into 'con' (false) and 'form' (self). Looking beyond the literal to the metaphorical is actually something we are familiar with in reading the meaning of our dreams. Few people take their dreams literally. For example, if you dream of an earthquake, you are unlikely to take that as a signal that you need to get the next plane out of the country, but instead you read the earthquake as the metaphorical representation of some major upheaval in your life.

We can apply the same kind of metaphorical approach to our everyday language that refers to body parts, body organs or bodily functions and, in so doing, we can find very powerful clues to the psychological intentions of any illness that may be present in our lives.

When you start to explore everyday language usage that involves the body, from the perspective of the intentions of the self in creating a particular illness, it is fascinating to see how frequently we use parts, organs and functions of the body to describe metaphorically emotional and psychological states. It makes sense that the self draws on these culturally agreed metaphors and locates the illness in the body part or organ or function that has the most common association with the psychological state that needs to be brought into the open. For example, the heart – a bodily organ – is commonly associated with love – a psychological state – and in our everyday language we speak metaphorically of being heart-broken, heart-sore, heartfelt, heart-scalded, hard-hearted, stout-hearted, to vividly describe emotional states. We speak of 'losing heart', of 'not having the heart to live', of 'dying of a broken heart'. It makes sense, then, that if a person has had to repress expression of his or her unconditional love for others or his or her need for unconditional love from others, the self might unconsciously choose the heart as the illness location that is most likely to draw attention to the 'love' disharmonies in the person's inner terrain that need to be resolved. Furthermore, the language the person uses to describe his or her heart symptoms will be meaningful in furthering the intentions of the self in bringing into the open the hidden psychological issues. For example, the person may speak of 'pressure' in his or her chest, or of 'the rhythm' of his or her heart being 'jumpy' or 'very uncomfortable', or of a 'sensation of tightness', or of a 'feeling of unreality' – all powerful metaphors for the state of his or her inner terrain, about which it is not safe for the person to speak openly.

It is important to emphasize that even though culturally we share common meanings, the intentions of the self in the specific language and location of the illness created are peculiar to the individual and reflect that individual's inner terrain. The generalized attachment of metaphorical meanings to particular illnesses obscures the marvellous creativity of the self in pursuing wholeness. Thus, in the example given above in relation to a heart illness, the metaphors described are meaningful for one of the authors but may not necessarily be meaningful for others who experience a heart illness.

Our intention in this chapter is to provide some signposts that will assist you in exploring the particular metaphorical meanings that may be present for you in: the location of an experienced illness; in the language you use to describe the symptoms of the illness; and in the everyday language that involves the particular body part or organ concerned. The value of exploring the psychological metaphors that may be involved is that it can assist in uncovering the compassionate intentions of your self in the illness.

Exploring the Links between Intentions and Language and Location

In exploring possible links between, on the one hand, the intentions of the self in the illness and, on the other hand, the metaphorical emotional meanings of the phrases we commonly use about the body part in question, it is helpful to be aware of the different organs of the body and their primary functions: vital organs, sense organs, support organs and body parts. Below we provide a number of examples of common, emotionally toned, linguistic associations for different parts of the body, in order to illustrate how these can provide very important clues as to why the self might choose a particular body part as the location for the substitute embodiment it has needed to create. We emphasize again that the examples given represent only possibilities; you will need to discover for yourself the emotional metaphors that are meaningful for you. We recognize that the examples of metaphorical meanings we give in the written page – although they come from our own experiences and those of people with whom we have been privileged to work – are a poor thing relative to the riches of information available when illness language and location are explored person-to-person with mindfulness of the complexity, depth and breadth of the contexts – inner and outer – within which the person is experiencing the illness.

Vital Organs

- the brain ('brainbox', 'brainless', 'brainy', 'brain-dead')
- the heart ('heartfelt', 'heart of stone', broken-hearted', 'heart-sick', 'at the heart of things')
- the blood ('red-blooded', 'bloodless', 'blue blood', 'makes my blood boil')
- the liver ('lily-livered', 'feeling liverish', 'a shiver in the liver', 'a jaundiced view')
- the lungs ('feel stifled', 'feel smothered', 'all choked up', 'it took my breath away').

Sense Organs

- the eyes ('the eyes are the window of the soul', 'he couldn't look me in the eye', 'blind to what's going on')
- the ears ('all ears', 'lend me an ear', 'deaf to my pleas')
- the nose ('being led by the nose, 'nosing around', 'sticking your nose in somebody else's business')
- the skin ('skin deep', 'thick-skinned', 'thin-skinned')
- the mouth ('no taste for living', 'mouthing off', 'close-mouthed').

Support Organs and Limbs

- the bladder ('her bladder is close to her eyes', 'what are you blathering on about?')
- the gall bladder ('how galling', 'full of bile')
- the genitals ('he has no balls', 'you prick') (Sadly, it is of note that the emotional metaphors associated with our genitals are often of such a demeaning nature.)
- the stomach ('can't stomach it', 'my stomach turned over')
- the intestines ('it stuck in my craw', 'I've had a bellyful of it', 'it went right through me')
- the muscles ('muscle-bound', 'tight')
- the teeth ('bite the bullet', 'once bitten, twice shy', 'get your teeth into it', 'I didn't put a tooth in it')
- the throat ('can't swallow that', 'caught in my throat')

Skeletal Parts

- the back ('back off', 'put your back into it', 'she has no backbone')
- the bones ('brittle', 'get to the bones of an issue')
- the feet ('stand on your own two feet', 'footloose', 'footless')
- the fingers and toes ('dig your nails into someone', 'nail-biting experience', 'I have my fingers in too many pies', 'get a grip')
- the hands ('hands off', 'the left hand doesn't know what the right hand is doing')
- the knees ('I'm on my knees', 'bend the knee', 'weak at the knees').

It would take a book in itself to examine the myriad ways in which different body parts and organs can be used metaphorically to represent different psychological states. What is crucial to recognize is that there are as many metaphors as there are people and the task of the professional helper (and of the persons themselves who are ill and exploring the intentions of their illnesses) is to listen closely to the words used to describe the location and symptoms of the illness.

Exploring Metaphor: Some Key Areas of the Body

In order to deepen familiarization with the link between the self's intentions and the metaphorical meaning of the language and location of illness, we have focused in the following sections on certain chosen body parts for more detailed exploration – the vital organs, the sense organs, the stomach and throat in the support organs, and the joints in the skeletal structure. Some parts of the body more than others appear to be associated in our culture with particular expressions of the self. We have noted where this appears to us to be the case, because it can provide important clues as to the particular features of self-expression that are being signalled by the illness as having had to be repressed. The purpose of the exploration is to become more alert to the clues provided by illness language and location as to what the self is signalling through the illness.

Vital Organs

When a vital organ is diseased, it seems very obvious to say that somehow what the self is signalling is that something 'vital' or 'critical' is at stake; that in some way 'vitality' and 'aliveness' are seriously blocked. The illness, in a substitute way, is drawing attention to the psychologically life-threatening situation and attempting to find resolution. An illness of a vital organ may also be the self signalling that the time is right for it to leave this world. The inner and outer contexts of the person who is ill would have to be explored thoroughly in order to reveal the particular intention of the illness.

BRAIN

The brain is a vital organ that is very much associated with intelligence and, indeed, many everyday phrases involving the brain appear to be connected with intellectual self-expression; this is worth bearing in mind when exploring the intentions of an illness located in the brain:

- 'he's got brains to burn'
- 'he hasn't a brain in his head'
- 'a brainless act'

- 'there's nothing in there'
- 'he's been brain-dead for years'
- 'use your brain'.

HEART

The language of the heart needs little introduction; its common association with love providing, perhaps, important clues as to the intentions of the self in heart disease. Organically, the heart is the physical pump of our life force (the blood). Symbolically, the heart represents the giving and receiving of the psycho-social-spiritual life force of love, of finding heart for self, and being in a heart place with others. For example:

- 'she's all heart'
- 'she's got a heart of gold'
- 'he's black-hearted'
- 'my heart stopped with fear'
- 'he lost heart'
- 'he's heartless'
- 'it gives me such a heart pain'
- 'the heart of the matter'
- 'I lost my heart to him'
- 'she is a heartache to me'
- 'I've no heart for it now'.

BLOOD

The vital function of blood flow around the body at a physical level can represent metaphorically the flow of life, of creative self-expression at the psychological level. Certain examples below suggest that diseases of the blood may be signalling interruptions to creative self-expression, but others also strongly suggest links with interruptions to social self-expression:

- 'my blood boils every time I see him'
- 'blood ties'
- 'blood brothers'
- 'bad blood' (between people)

- 'my blood ran cold with fear'
- 'there's blood on your hands'
- 'red-blooded male'
- 'blood is thicker than water'
- 'he wants to draw blood'
- 'blood feud'
- 'hot-blooded'
- 'bloody-minded'.

LUNGS

Air is what connects every living thing, for without it we would all perish; perhaps, then, illness of the lungs is intended by the self to signal something crucial to our survival. Taking one's first breath is the infant's first act of physical separation, of freedom from the physically symbiotic union with the mother; psychologically, separateness is also a crucial issue for us as human beings. In so many of the ancient languages the word 'breath' meant 'spirit' or 'soul'. It may also be an important clue to the self's intention in lung disease to remember that the intake of breath is referred to as 'inspiration' – also the word for creativity – and exhalation of breath is referred to as 'expiration' – the word 'expire' also meaning 'to let go'. Some examples of metaphorical language associated with 'air' and 'breath' are:

- 'coming up for air'
- 'gasping for air'
- 'I feel all choked up'
- 'I feel stifled in this company'
- (giving herself) 'airs and graces'
- 'inflated' ego
- 'all puffed up'
- 'takes one's breath away'
- 'can't catch my breath, I'm so busy'
- 'I'm gasping at her audacity'.

Holding our breath is a natural response to stress or shock; we have come across several instances of adults who can trace the onset of childhood illness to the 'shock' experience of a parent's crossness or harshness, or to the 'shock' experience of witnessing their parents fighting.

LIVER

The word 'liver' describes a bodily organ but also describes a way of being in the world – a 'liver' of life. In many ways the psycho-social meaning of the word fits with one of the main functions of the liver – the storage and distribution of energy – and, perhaps, gives clues as to the self's intention in liver disease. The liver also has a detoxi-fication function, whereby foreign poisons either taken in from outside or produced by the body itself are de-activated. Some examples of metaphorical language associated with the liver are:

- 'he's lily-livered'
- 'she has a very jaundiced view of the world'
- 'a poisonous look'
- 'full of venom'.

Sense Organs

Metaphorically, the sense organs may be taken to represent our 'sensitivity' to what is happening to us in the different worlds we inhabit. The examples below of metaphorical language associated with the sense organs suggest a strong link with the self's social expression and so, perhaps, diseases of the sense organs may be signalling interruptions to this domain of self-expression.

EYES

- 'love is blind'
- 'look me straight in the eye'
- 'she has no "in-sight" into herself'
- 'what the eye doesn't see, the heart won't feel'
- 'an eye for an eye, a tooth for a tooth'
- 'a dirty look'.

EARS

- 'I'm all ears'
- 'keep your ear to the ground'

- 'deaf to the world'
- 'turning a deaf ear to'
- 'I got an earful from her'.

NOSE

- 'she has a nose for gossip'
- 'she keeps putting her nose into other people's business'
- 'nose to the grindstone'
- 'nosy parker'
- 'he gets up my nose'.

TOUCH

- 'touchy-feely'
- 'out of touch'
- 'soft touch'
- 'touching you up'
- 'kick for touch'.

TASTE

- 'no taste for life'
- 'that's tasteless behaviour'
- 'that's in bad taste'
- 'I'll give you a "taste" of your own medicine'.

Skin

The most common metaphorical phrases involving the skin are: 'thin-skinned'; 'thick-skinned'; 'skin-deep'; 'get under your skin'; 'skin alive'; and 'saving our skins'. The skin reveals so much of what goes on psychologically in us. We perspire with fear ('get into a sweat'), go red with embarrassment, go white with shock, 'flush' with excitement, get 'goose pimples', break out in 'rashes'.

Support Organs

Among the support organs, we have selected here the stomach and the throat for further elaboration.

STOMACH

The key function of the stomach is to receive and digest what it has taken in through eating. Analogically, we need to 'digest' what we receive psychologically from the world outside; and register the feelings that arise and nourish ourselves with what is good and resolve any conflict that may arise. This, of course, is easier said than done in social systems where it can be highly threatening to disagree or express your own opinion or bring a conflict out into the open. It may be, then, that stomach illnesses are an important substitute means for the self to reveal interruptions to emotional self-expression. Some clues to the intentions of the self in illnesses of the stomach – such as indigestion, peptic ulcers (gastric or duodenal), cancer – lie in the following commonly used phrases:

- 'he's gutless'
- 'I feel all churned up inside'
- 'I feel sick any time I think about it'
- 'I've no appetite for arguing'
- 'I'm full of fear'
- 'comfort eating'
- 'biting off more than you can chew'
- 'worry guts'
- 'you make me sick'
- 'she's always belly-aching'
- 'I have butterflies in my stomach at the thought of it'.

THROAT

The following are some examples of metaphorical references to the throat that give clues as to the possible intentions of the self in throat illnesses, such as inflamed throat, laryngitis, cancer:

- 'a lump in the throat'
- 'some people would swallow anything'
- 'fed up to the back teeth'
- 'that's hard to swallow'
- 'just cannot swallow it any more'

- 'swallow hard before you do it'
- 'choked with emotion'
- 'cough it up, whatever is bothering you'.

Skeletal Parts

The phrase 'skeletons in the closet' is a vivid example of the use of the bone structure of the body as a metaphorical representation of a psycho-social condition. Phrases such as 'make no bones about it', getting to the 'bones of the matter', being 'bone tired' are further examples of the outer physical structure acting as metaphor for the inner psychological state. It appears from the examples given below of typical metaphorical associations of the skeletal structure that illnesses in these bodily parts may be signalling interruptions of the self's behavioural expression. Many examples of the 'back' as metaphor have already been given but 'spineless' is a particularly vivid example. In regard to the shoulders, metaphorical phrases such as 'shouldering responsibility', 'shouldering the blame', 'taking a lot on your shoulders', 'shoulder somebody out of the way' are familiar to us, as is the supportive metaphor of 'shoulder to shoulder'. The neck has several associated metaphorical phrases – for example, 'putting your neck on the line', having a 'rubber neck', being a 'pain in the neck', having got 'some neck', 'sticking your neck out'. The head, in particular, has many metaphorical associations; the examples below suggesting a connection with the psychological need to take charge openly in one's life:

- 'he lives in his head'
- 'he's so headstrong'
- 'she's so pig-headed'
- 'use your head'
- 'headed in the wrong direction'
- 'I need to get my head together on this'
- 'she's empty-headed'
- 'I'm just beating my head off a stone wall here'.

The limbs, particularly the hands and feet, are often used in everyday language as powerful metaphorical representations of deeper issues in one's inner terrain:

- 'hands on'
- 'hands up'
- 'sleight of hand'
- 'one hand doesn't know what the other hand is doing'
- 'hand in glove'
- 'hand to mouth'
- 'a lot in hand'
- 'tight-fisted'
- 'stand on your own two feet'
- 'steady on your feet'
- 'go out feet first'
- 'best foot forward'
- 'wrong-footed'
- 'footloose and fancy free'
- 'feet off the ground'
- 'he has two left feet'
- 'digging your heels in'.

JOINTS

It is the joints that provide mobility, flexibility and dexterity; a stiffening of the joints symbolically may represent being 'stiff', 'rigid', 'inflexible', 'stubborn', 'entrapped', having 'no room to move'. We mentioned the shoulders already and the common medical condition of a 'frozen shoulder' may be symbolically indicative of a 'stuckness' that requires attention.

ELBOW

Needing 'elbow room' and 'elbowing somebody out of the way' could be significant metaphors for needing our own space and the threats that occur when that space is invaded. When that invasiveness is not consciously dealt with, it may embody itself in conditions such as tennis elbow.

HIP

The phrase 'joined at the hip' describes the serious psychological situation whereby one's stability is tied up with another person (parent, spouse, offspring or employer). This is an example of how a commonly used phrase can provide a clue as to the possible underlying intention of illness – in this case, disease of the hip.

KNEE

One of the present authors underwent a cartilage operation some years ago. At the time he put the condition down to tennis playing, but now realizes that it represented a time in his life when he very much 'bent the knee' to other people's needs, demands, expectations. He also recalls 'knee-jerk' reactions to conflict, coming from disharmonies in his inner terrain; disharmonies that he now realizes were being signalled by his self through the physical problem with his knee.

Intentions and the Verbal Description of Symptoms: Exploring the Link

Very often the language we use to describe our illness symptoms metaphorically represents the deeper intentions of the illness, and so an examination of these verbal descriptions can give vital clues as to what needs to be done at a real and conscious level. You will recall that the illness is the substitute for the real response that you dare not openly express. Substitute responses arise from fear, while real responses arise from unconditional love. An example that illustrates the amazing creativity of the self in its use of language is the many ways in which different individuals can describe the experience of a headache:

- 'throbbing'
- 'piercing'
- 'dull'
- 'splitting'
- 'pounding'

- 'sharp'
- 'blinding'
- 'pressure behind my eyes'
- 'causing a fuzzy feeling'.

The location of the symptom – the head – may, in itself, point to being too much 'in your head', or the need to be always 'ahead' of others. The particular description of the experience of the headache gives further clues. For example, a throbbing headache may represent a relentless criticism of yourself in order to ensure that you offset criticism from others – a substitute means of maintaining wholeness. The throbbing headache could also be representing your going over and over in your head some hurt, disappointment or failure, or it could be pointing to the need for much more attention to be paid to unresolved hurts and the need to nurture yourself – to get to a heart place with yourself. The piercing headache could symbolize the feeling of being cut to the quick by another's response to you and the need to penetrate – to get through to – your own unique worth and goodness. A dull headache may symbolize the lack of excitement in your life and the need to access the adventurous side of your nature. A splitting headache may represent being split away from your true self – a situation of divided loyalties, where enmeshment with others has become a substitute for the real need for self-reliance. A pounding headache may symbolize the constant pressurizing of yourself to get things right or to please others or to prevent failure or to prove yourself. A sharp headache may represent the cutting, everyday experience of somebody close to you being 'sharp' with you and the emotional hurt experienced. A blinding headache may indicate the inner emotional pressure to blind yourself to certain harsh realities that would be perilous to reveal. The description of a headache as causing pressure behind the eyes may be a representation of some pressing issue that needs to be seen and acknowledged. The experience of a fuzzy feeling may be bringing attention to a lack of clarity in your life – a protection of not bringing into focus something that is causing disharmony in your inner terrain. Noticing the thoughts – perhaps even writing them out – that may be flooding your mind prior to the onset of the headache and during the headache can give you a good sense of what is happening in your inner world and offer some valuable clues as to the deeper emotional ache that the headache is signalling.

The multilayered meaning of language reflects the immense creativity of the self in communicating in masked ways what is not yet safe to communicate in direct and conscious ways. Take the example of the manager asked to deliver a presentation to executive managers; he creatively develops 'a sore throat' and in a croaking voice says, 'I've lost my voice'. How powerful this metaphor is – 'I've lost my voice' – for the situation where the individual as a child had to silence his voice in the face of strict and hypercritical authority figures. When a similar threat reappears in adulthood, and separateness has not yet been found, illness can present itself as an additional substitute response that might succeed in eliminating the threat and maintaining wholeness.

In exploring your verbal descriptions of your symptoms, it is important to remember that there is no set meaning that applies in all cases; the task is to determine the specific meaning that applies in your particular experience. Exploration of the contexts of what has gone before – for example, an embarrassing experience – or what is present – for example, being faced with aggression from another – or what is to follow – for example, getting married shortly – will help in the process of interpreting the metaphors that are present for you.

With a view to deepening your sense of the creative wisdom involved in the language used for illnesses, we provide below some further examples of how the description of symptoms provides powerful clues to the underlying issues involved. Stomach problems, like headaches, are a common complaint. It is our experience that very often the intention of stomach pain is to draw attention to underlying fears and the need to reclaim fearlessness. Some typical examples of the verbal descriptions of stomach pain are:

- 'I've a pain in my gut'
- 'My tummy is upset'
- 'I feel like I want to get sick'

- 'I feel all knotted up inside'
- 'I've a burning sensation in my insides'
- 'I'm full of acid'
- 'It feels like something is twisting my gut'
- 'I can't keep anything down'
- 'I feel violently sick'.

Some examples of the kind of emotionally significant queries that these symptom descriptions could point to:

- What gut (crucial) issue is being flagged here?
- What is the set way of doing things that requires overturning?
- What is the sickness in your relationship with yourself that needs to be resolved?
- In what situation, or with whom, are you in a knot?
- What is the burning issue that is calling out for attention?
- What is the acid test that needs to be carried out?
- In what ways are you getting yourself into a twist for others?
- What is it that you are not presently prepared to digest?
- What is the violence you are doing to yourself that demands urgent addressing?

The Importance of Context

Clearly, an understanding of the context in which metaphorical language involving the body occurs is critical to uncovering the particular underlying meaning and intention of illness for the individual involved. Take, for example, the woman with a knee complaint for whom the phrase 'can't stand on her own two feet' has a particular resonance. The context may be physical – for example, she has lost all power in her legs – or it may be psychological – she has little or no hold on self or life – or it may be sociological – she experiences people as letting her down all the time. The context may also be spiritual – life is experienced by her as being meaningless. The exact location of the condition and the pain and other symptoms are highly significant factors, as are the circumstances of the

When, the Where, the What and the Who. For example, the woman may find that she has to 'bend the knee' to unrealistic demands; these unrealistic demands occur in the workplace; and the demands occur in her relationship with her boss. The intention of the self in creating the substitute response of the knee complaint requires a deeper examination, the intention always lying in the realm of the shadow self. For example, the woman may have had to repress expression of her own needs, preferences, priorities; she may have learned in early relationships that in order to be any way safe in her world, she needed to bend the knee to those on whom she was dependent for love. The importance of context is discussed more fully in the next chapter.

6 Steps to Uncovering the Intentions of Illness

Uncovering Intentions: A Sensitive Process

The aim of this chapter is to provide some guidelines on how to uncover the intentions of an illness. The self is wise and may reveal only part of the picture to begin with, but the longest journey starts with the first solid steps. Because the intentions lie in the unconscious domain, bringing these into conscious awareness, more often than not, is a deep and sensitive process.

Uncovering intentions is a deep process because the underlying hidden issues that the self is intending to bring forward through the illness are likely to have long roots, most usually stretching right back to childhood. It is not for nothing that the phrase 'the Hero's Journey' has been used to refer to the process of facing directly the hurts, the terrors, the unmet needs, the neglects and abandonment that we can suffer in our early lives; the often very painful, but necessary, process that brings us back home to the place of responsiveness, the place of loving kindness in action, the place of unconditional love. Of course, uncovering the intentions of a particular illness is not always so deep or complex; sometimes the intentions can be close to the surface of consciousness and the journey is more straightforward and easier to travel.

Uncovering intentions is a sensitive process because, as explored in Chapters 2 and 3, it is the very lack of safety that led, in the first place, to the repressions of self-expression that necessitated the substitute response of illness. Safety, because it is about unconditional love, is an issue that arises in relationship. Accordingly, how others around us relate to us in our illness is a highly significant influence on whether or not we feel secure enough to explore the underlying intentions (the kind of caring relationships that promote safety are discussed in Chapter 9).

In attempting to uncover intentions, it is wise to 'start at the edges'; perhaps a safe start-point being to collect information on the external context of the illness – the when, where, with whom, how often, how severe, how enduring, kind of questions. The more information that is gathered about and around the illness, the more likely it is that an accurate assessment of the intentions of the illness will be made. But any interpretation is best treated as a hypothesis that needs to be reality-tested. When an interpretation emerges around which you experience that intuitive sense of 'that's it, that makes total sense', then it is highly likely that you are on the right path to recovery of what has lain repressed in the shadow world. The best reality test is whether your conscious action in response to your sense of the illness's intentions actually leads to a greater sense of inner harmony. Of course, responsiveness to uncovered intentions is not a once-off or a quick matter; responding with loving care and commitment to the underlying hidden fears, hurts and threats is a long-term affair and its results may only clearly emerge in the longterm. The more safety and support you have in the different worlds you inhabit, the more likely it is that you will be empowered to persist with the loving responsiveness that restores you to knowing and experiencing your wholeness. Ultimately, healing is about realization. It is the conscious taking up of the loving tasks signalled unconsciously by the illness as being necessary that leads to the lifting of the repressions in the inner terrain, the emergence of open, real self-expression, and the return to wholeness.

Steps Involved in Uncovering Intentions

We outline below the kind of steps we see as being involved in undergoing the conscious attempt to understand the intentions of any illness that may arise in your life. In understanding the queries involved in the thirteen steps, you may want to revert to previous chapters; we have noted the relevant chapters for different steps. It may not always be necessary to go through all the steps; sometimes the information gained from completing the earlier steps is sufficient to enable you to realize the self's intentions without any need to delve further. If it happens that you go through all the steps and no realization occurs – no enlightenment on intentions – it may be that you need to seek further support within a safe environment. As you will see, some of the steps are relatively straightforward and the answers to the queries involved in the steps much more accessible. You need to be patient with yourself and have understanding and compassion for the fact that some of the queries involved are deep and complex and need to be approached with sensitivity. The steps are as follows:

1. What is the nature of the presenting symptoms?
2. Where are the symptoms located in the body? Are there any particular phrases in your everyday language that are associated with the body part in question? If so, what psychological/emotional state do these phrases metaphorically represent? (See Chapter 5.)
3. How, in your own words, would you describe the symptoms you are experiencing? (See Chapter 5 for the clues your descriptions may give.)
4. What significant life events were happening *before* the onset of the illness?
5. Is there any significant life event due to occur in the near future?
6. What words would you use to best describe what is currently going on in your *inner* world? That is, how you feel within yourself, how at ease you are in yourself or what disharmonies you may be experiencing. (See Chapters 2 and 3.)
7. What is currently going on in your *outer* world, in the environments that are significant for you, such as family, marriage, workplace, community? How would you describe the nature of the relationships with the significant others in your life? What threats may be present for you in those relationships? (See Chapter 3.)

8. What is it that the illness is making you do?
9. What is it that the illness stops you from doing?
10. What threats/disharmonies in your inner terrain could your self be trying to signal through the illness that is not safe to bring forward directly? (See Chapter 3.)
11. What particular domain of self-expression could it be that the illness is flagging as having been repressed? (See Chapter 1.)
12. What realization of unconditional love, of wholeness, is the self pushing into consciousness through the illness?
13. What are the loving, real, open actions you need consciously to take to maintain wholeness and the place of unconditional love?

It may be that you find it difficult to discover the answers to the queries involved in the steps. This is understandable and wise, since it can be threatening for us to touch into our inner turmoil and, at times, it is necessary for us to seek the help of others – friend, family member, professional carer – who can provide the necessary safety, loving kindness and compassionate understanding that will make it safe to explore the intentions of illness.

A Story of the Intentions of an Illness

The following story of a young woman, who presented with 'fainting spells', may help put flesh on the bare bones of the thirteen steps. This young woman had been hospitalized a number of times and innumerable tests had been carried out to determine the causes of these blackouts. Epilepsy was mooted, but the symptoms were not typical of epilepsy. None of the tests led to discovery of a physical basis for the problem. A psychogenic cause – hysteria – was then mooted but without any explanation as to what that really meant. The fainting spells continued. When she first met with one of the present authors and was asked to describe her experience of her fainting spells, she used a phrase – 'when I fitted' – that immediately gave a very strong clue with regard to the underlying repressed issues. The therapist asked, 'Fitted in what way?' Seeing the metaphor in her phrase, the young woman replied, 'Fitted into what everybody wants of me.' The therapist then asked, 'And what happens when you "fit" yourself to everybody else's needs?' She responded, 'I lose all sense of who I am.'

Her embodiment had very cleverly captured her repressions of her own individuality and her right to live her own life – very necessary repressions in the face of threats in important relationships. Her slip of the tongue, 'when I fitted', was an ingenious, unconscious creation of her self to test the waters of the therapeutic relationship as to whether or not it would be safe enough to begin the journey of uncovering the intentions of the illness. If her slip of the tongue had not been taken up, understood and responded to, then the illness would have continued without discovery of its intentions.

In applying the thirteen steps and queries outlined above, the purposes of the young woman's illness become even more apparent:

1. Her condition: fainting without warning, passing out, losing consciousness. Metaphorically, these physical experiences represented her own loss of contact with herself; her loss of conscious self-expression.

2. Symptom location: in her whole body; her body went weak and she passed out. The location suggested a total, all-over repression of self-expression.

3. She talked of the fainting in the wonderful slip of the tongue 'when I fitted'.

4. Before the onset of the symptoms, she had read a book about a young woman who had felt entrapped by her parents' problems. This turned out to be an important precedent to the subsequent 'fits'. Somehow, the story provided some level of safety – support from the understanding she saw expressed by the author of the book – to consider her own situation.

5. A change was looming in her work world – she was looking out for a professional post. This emerged as significant because she was not at all ready to leave home and to be independent, and the emergence of this insecurity

accounted for the rather sudden onset of the fainting spells.

6. She felt she always had to be there for her mother and that it would be selfish of her to leave home. She felt her mother would 'fall apart' (an important metaphor in her case) without her, but it was clear that it was she herself who was 'falling apart'.

7. She was attending an intensive self-development course. Others on this course had shared their different repressions and inner disharmonies and the group provided strong and safe support for the embodiment to be understood for what it was – a substitute response to threats in her world.

8. The illness made her attend to herself and to her having 'fitted' all her life. It was amazing for her to see that her symptoms mirrored so accurately the repressions that had occurred and that her self was valiantly attempting to counter, albeit in a substitute physical manner.

9. The illness led to her being hospitalized, so that it stopped her 'fitting in' to the needs of the family. It also provided the opportunity for reflection on what was happening to her.

10. The embodiment was drawing attention to the threats of rejection by her mother were she to express directly and clearly the need to be independent and separate.

11. The repressions being brought to light were the loss of self-expression and the right to live her own life – and the bringing to light of this was eloquently done!

12. The realization was for her to take responsibility for her own life and separate out (the 'fall apart' metaphor here was significant for her) from taking responsibility for others. This was her greatest and most difficult challenge but the strong support that the self-development group provided helped her to own and be responsive to this crucial matter.

13. The actions needed were for her to be attentive to herself and to fly the home-nest (the family as womb-world) and find her home within herself (the self as womb-world) – actions that she eventually managed very well to implement.

In addition to the relief of the psychological inner disharmony, there was also physical relief for this young woman: once she realized how she had creatively 'fitted in' to the needs of her parents – and responded to that realization – no more fainting spells occurred. Of course, if she had not consciously taken charge of redressing the interruptions to self-expression that had occurred for her, there is little doubt that the fainting would have recurred, or some other, even more powerful, embodiment would have developed.

Making Sense of the Information Gathered

As you will have seen in the previous chapter, it is at the metaphorical level that the self tells the story behind the illness. It is important to bear this in mind when you are trying to make sense of the information you gather through the thirteen steps, particularly with regard to steps 1 to 3. If, for example, your presenting symptom is the common complaint of back pain, it may be that, as previously suggested, your self is trying to bring forward that you are taking too much on your back, or you are not having sufficient support. Your answers, in this case, to question 8 – what is it that the illness is making you do? – may be that when you get the pain, you are compelled to seek support, even if it is the substitute support of an orthopaedic mattress or a straight-backed chair!

Another common condition is migraine headache. Migraine sufferers frequently speak of the headaches as affecting one side of the head and occurring suddenly; the headache is often found to be accompanied by stomach or digestive symptoms, such as vomiting or diarrhoea. Relief from the physical symptoms, is often sought by being alone in bed in a darkened room. If this were your presenting symptom, your answers to questions 10 and 11 – what repression is being brought into the light? – might be that what the self is metaphorically bringing out through the one-sided headache is the defensive strategy you have had to develop of being 'one-sided', being rigid, seeing only your own point of view. The symptom of vomiting may be the self's means of representing not being able to stomach an opposing view, and the diarrhoea may represent the fear that is there ('in the shit') when you experience opposition from others. The need to be alone may serve the purpose of removing yourself from whatever is threatening you, and wanting to be in a darkened room may serve the purpose of hiding your vulnerability and securing the response from others of 'being left alone'. Such responses to the physical symptoms can bring relief from the migraine headache but something further is required for relief of the inner psychological discomfort. In answering question 6 – what is going on in your inner world? – it could be useful to consider the nature of the thoughts currently in your head, what you may be worrying your head about, and in what aspect of your life is the worry occurring – sexual, emotional, social, work-related, intellectual? You may discover that you are 'beating your head off a stone wall' in regard to something that really matters to you.

Heart disease is one of the most common causes of death in our society. If this should be your presenting symptom, it could be valuable to bear in mind that the heart lies at the centre of the body, beating rhythmically without any conscious effort on our part. Heart 'dis-ease' may mean that your natural (love) rhythm has been disturbed. The common metaphors around the heart – soft-hearted, hard-hearted, heartless, heart-scalded, heart-broken – can give you help in answering questions 11 and 12, concerned with realization of the required resolution.

The information gained from questions 4 and 5 – concerned with events before the onset of the illness and events perceived as likely to occur in the near future – can provide important answers as to the catalyst to the present occurrence of the embodiment. Some examples of events preceding the occurrence of an embodiment are: the breakdown of an intimate relationship, change of job, examination failure. Some examples of future events that can be associated with onset of illness are: marriage, academic examination, mother-in-law coming to stay, presentation to colleagues at work. Some possible metaphors that may be operating in the above examples are: 'breakdown' (perhaps of inner harmony), 'change' (perhaps fear of change), 'failure' (perhaps the failure to express your whole self), 'marriage' (perhaps absence of inner union), 'examination' (perhaps identification of self with performance), 'mother-in-law visit' (perhaps not being a mother to yourself) and 'presentation' (perhaps not being present to yourself).

The answers to questions 6 and 7 – concerning your inner and outer worlds – can often reveal a lack of 'innerness' and an addiction to what others think. When you consider that the most common addiction is the addiction to what others think (a wise substitute response in the face of threats to self-expression), these two questions can be critical to understanding the self's intentions in the illness.

The answers to questions 8 to 11 provide powerful information on what the self is attempting to bring forward into conscious awareness. Suppose your presenting symptom is a 'blinding headache'; it may be that it stops you from pressurizing yourself and makes you nurture and rest yourself in a way you would not normally do. The 'blinding headache' may be bringing forward the neglect of yourself that you have protectively developed, as this is reflected in your punishing and pressuring behaviour towards yourself. The adjective 'blinding' may represent your emotional blindness towards yourself. The point of question 10 is to try to discover what it is that you need which you are seeking in a substitute way through the illness; the answers here leading on to question 11, which is concerned with discovering what expressions of the self have had to be repressed and lie hidden in the shadow world. One possibility here, in the case of the 'blinding' headache, is: being loved conditionally for achievements but, tragically, not for self.

The last two questions are concerned with uncovering what it is you now consciously need to see and do to return to wholeness, to create the safeties that will enable you to give open, direct, real expression to whatever aspects of self you have had to repress. It is this responsiveness to the intentions of the illness, this conscious adoption of responsibility for your well-being, which brings the substitute job of the illness to a close.

A Story of Unfolding Information on Intentions

A story from the life of one of the present authors, recounted below, may serve to illustrate the unfolding of information as one goes through the thirteen steps.

> My presenting symptom was that I had begun to bring up blood from my lungs. Hospitalization and a week of tests did not detect any physical basis. The location of the condition – the lungs – indicated a constriction in breathing my own life. I was twenty-four years of age, three months away from ordination into the priesthood (future event looming), and had become a deacon at the time of onset of the condition (prior event). I was practising Catholicism and co-celebrating Mass, even though I no longer believed. I recall describing the condition as 'I am bringing up blood'; bringing to mind for me metaphors such as 'blood is thicker than water'. In my case, I was protectively allowing 'blood ties' to block my true self-expression. What was going on in my inner world was the turmoil of living a lie and being terrified of letting down my parents and others. In my outer world, there were great expectations of me but these expectations far exceeded my own perceptions of my capacities at the time. The illness made me pay attention to and talk about 'blood' and it meant I had to go to hospital and so out of the monastery. It stopped me from living a hypocritical existence.
>
> Through the embodiment I was able to talk about an apparent serious threat to my physical well-being, at a time when I was not yet ready to talk consciously about the serious threat to my psychological well-being; the real need being to break the 'blood ties' and be honest and authentic (which came soon afterwards). The physical possibility of there being 'a shadow on my lungs' metaphorically represented the repression in the shadow world that needed to be brought into the open – the threats that were there preventing me from living my own life. My defensive belief was that I *should* only be there for others. The realization was that I deserved to be there for myself and that the one responsibility I could take, and needed to take, was for my own life. This required cutting the blood ties that bound me.

7 Uncovering Intentions:
Adult Illnesses

Creating the Necessary Safety

You will be aware from the previous chapter that the kinds of query involved in the process of uncovering the intentions of the self in illness are deep and far-reaching. In order to engage in the process, you need to feel that you are in a safe emotional environment; this safety arising from how you are with yourself and how others around you are relating to you in your illness. When your illness symptoms are not major, you can often figure out for yourself what underlying meaning the illness has for you, but there can also be times of serious or life-threatening illness when you need the guidance and support of another – perhaps a professional – to work through the process. Whether you are working through the process on your own or with another, the crucial factor is that there is honouring of the wisdom in your illness; that there is respect for you as the one with the answers; that there is recognition that these answers are particular to your individual case; and that there is commitment to carrying out whatever particular actions emerge as being necessary to resolve the particular issues that arise for you.

Making it safe for you to approach the process means creating an environment of kindness, patience and sensitivity. You are likely to need a lot of support – from within yourself and from others around you. It needs to be taken into account that by the very nature of illness you are already in a vulnerable place physically. You are having to attend to yourself on several fronts – physical, emotional, social and, perhaps, spiritual. It is not easy to have to deal with several fronts at the one time, but that, in truth, is what the occurrence of illness is calling out for. When we are ill, we need to have all the stops pulled out in our care; illness is a very powerful alerting signal from the self with regard to the need to safeguard our wholeness.

Because the intentions of illness – as with all substitute behaviours – lie below consciousness, the uncovering process involves us picking up whatever clues we can. But the amazing thing is that once we understand that the language of the unconscious is metaphorical, and once we start becoming more familiar with this language, we discover that the self is extraordinarily ingenious in creating very powerful signposts for what has had to lie hidden. You will have seen in Chapter 5 the rich store of information that can be available to us when we explore the possible metaphorical meanings of the function of the body part involved in the illness, of the common language associated with the body part, and of the language we use to describe our symptoms. Remember the impetus of the self is always towards wholeness, towards maintaining the place of unconditional love, and so the result of the uncovering process is discovery of what is needed for your compassionate care.

Our purpose in this chapter is to provide further opportunities to deepen your skill in reading the available clues about the underlying hidden disharmonies and conflicts that should be brought into the light; opportunities to become more skilled in interpreting the metaphors that can be involved in the illness itself, in the location of the illness, in the language associated with the body part in question, and in your verbal description of the symptoms you are experiencing. We provide below some case illustrations of intentions with regard to some of the more frequent symptoms experienced by adults. Of necessity, these case illustrations have been greatly summarized and simplified, but we emphasize that the uncovering process, that interpreting metaphor, is not a simplistic process, and it is only when the contexts surrounding the person who is ill are fully explored that the riches of information that are actually present become available.

Some Common Adult Illnesses: Possible Intentions

Among the leading causes of death in our society are heart disease, cancer, cirrhosis of the liver, lung ailments, accidental injuries and suicide. The more common symptoms of which adults complain are back pain, headaches, stomach problems, constipation, insomnia, high or low blood pressure, arthritis, irritable bowel syndrome, high cholesterol, conjunctivitis, tinnitus, tachycardia, asthma, recurring infections and headaches. In earlier chapters we have given case illustrations of the intentions of the self underlying individuals' experiences of back pain, fainting spells and migraine headaches. Here, we provide further opportunities for practice in uncovering intentions through exploration of cases of high blood pressure, irritable bowel syndrome, tinnitus, cancer and heart disease.

Stress as an Alerting Signal

Stress symptoms constitute one of the most obvious ways that the self expresses threats to well-being, and the consequent need for the creation of substitute responses. But, sadly, most people protectively regard stress symptoms as something that 'happens to me' rather than as something 'I create' in my wisdom. In your daily life, it may seem that pressure and strain occur from the time you wake in the morning and your thoughts turn to, for example, all the jobs you have to do in the day, being stuck in morning traffic, being pushed and jostled by others, conflict with a work colleague, work deadlines, marriage difficulties, obligations to family of origin. Initially, stress manifests itself physically at the level of symptoms such as aches, pains, feelings of pressure in the head, breathlessness, back pain, shoulder pain. But if the underlying psycho-social issues are not recognized and addressed, the physical symptoms can escalate to more serious manifestations, such as irritable bowel syndrome, heart disease, lung ailments, stomach ulcers, thyroid difficulties, multiple sclerosis (MS), motor neurone disease (MN) and myalgic encephalomyelitis (ME). These escalations are wisely created by the self when the earlier substitute responses – the less severe physical symptoms – have not been powerful enough to withstand the ongoing threats to well-being. As with all substitute responses, the more severe illnesses have but one purpose, and this a compassionate purpose – for you to realize your wholeness and live consciously from that solid inner terrain.

An environment of safety (see Chapter 2) allows you to respond to stress symptoms as a wise creation and as a push from the self for the resolution of existing threats to well-being. When viewed as a creation of the self, rather than being the problem, the stress symptoms become opportunities to uncover the real problem. For example, the early wakening to worries about 'all I have to do' can become the realization of the need to deepen my sense of self-reliance and not allow external activities to rule my life. Rushing for the train can mirror the reality that you lose sight of your sacred presence and can be pointing to the need to give more time to yourself. Worry about being stuck in traffic can be a metaphor for 'being stuck' in a pattern of behaviour that protectively has put everything else before care of self; the intention being to effect the realization that unless you put care of yourself as a priority, the resulting inner conflict may need to be expressed through ill health. Our first responsibility – and only feasible responsibility – is for ourselves; it is only when we fulfil that critical responsibility that we can then act responsibly towards others, and provide the care and support that will enable them to take responsibility for themselves. 'Deadlines' can be a powerful metaphor for the extremes of neglect of our physical and emotional health that we will sometimes go to in order to meet some work or study requirements. It is a dark culture, whether in the world of work or education, that supports, and indeed often praises, such neglect – and it is this darkness that the self may be bringing to light through the stress symptoms. The realization needed is for us to reclaim our lives and not sacrifice them to the protective illusion that success brings about inner harmony and fulfilment.

Stress symptoms, then, are a tool of the self to signal the actions needed to realize consciously and express wholeness. When, through lack of safety, you deny, ignore or dismiss the signs and effects of stress, the risk to health increases and the ill health itself becomes an even stronger call from the self for the resolution of inner psycho-social conflicts. Resolution lies in conscious realization and open expression of care of self.

Blood Pressure Problems

Blood pressure problems – either hypotension or hypertension – are common ailments among adults; these being referred to as essential hypo-/hypertension when no physical cause can be identified. It appears that most blood pressure problems are essential in nature. In using the word 'essential' as a descriptive term for certain instances of blood pressure problems, medical experts, perhaps unwittingly, are pointing towards the possibility that the occurrence of blood pressure problems is a metaphorical representation of the repression of some essential expression of self; this would make sense in the context that blood, both literally and symbolically, is the medium of life.

In our work with people experiencing low or high blood pressure we have noticed that the psycho-social processes the person exhibits often parallel the physical processes involved in the particular blood pressure problem. For people experiencing low blood pressure, the kinds of hidden issue that emerged for them as being signalled by the hypotension tended to be concerned with avoidance of challenge, with withdrawal from conflict, with renunciation of power. One person, for example, discovered that instances of loss of consciousness often occurred at times of conflict; any hint of conflict posed great threat for her, left her feeling 'weak at the knees', and fainting, by causing distraction, served the unconscious purpose of giving her 'permission' to withdraw from the conflict situation. Some other examples of the hidden issues that emerged as being signalled by the low blood pressure problem were the sense of: 'being unable to stand up for myself'; 'being unable to stand the pace'; 'being unable to stand on my own two feet'. High blood pressure often appears to accompany the psycho-social process of continuous anxiety about life tasks or situations that are not being resolved for the person. Some clients with high blood pressure have identified for themselves a tendency to use the substitute response of 'busyness' to protect against the threat involved in resolving the difficulties in their lives.

Individuals with low and high blood pressure are similar, in that both feel highly threatened by conflict, but whereas those with low blood pressure resort to taking refuge in non-action, those with high blood pressure tend to take refuge in diversionary action. It is of note that low blood pressure is more common in women, for whom passivity is often more socially acceptable than mature self-assertion; whereas high blood pressure is more common among men, from whom aggressive expression of frustration is often tolerated in society. In both cases, the needed realization being signalled by the symptoms is the open take-up of their power for purposeful action, directed clearly at their unmet needs.

A Story of Uncovering the Intentions of High Blood Pressure

John, a teacher in his late twenties, was referred with essential hypertension by his GP, who felt he would benefit from hypnosis, or from learning some relaxation or meditation techniques. In helping the young man, the essential task for the therapist was to create the safety for him to understand himself, not as a victim of the illness, but as a wise creator, so that he might then be able to engage in the process of uncovering the compassionate intentions of the illness and realize the real actions that were needed to resolve the underlying psycho-social conflicts. The following account is what emerged from the thirteen-query process.

1. *What was the nature of the presenting symptoms?*
This young teacher had been diagnosed by his medical practitioner as having essential hypertension, duodenal ulcer and early morning diarrhoea and vomiting.

2. *Where in the body were the symptoms located?*
The answer here was quite straightforward – the blood flow, the head, the stomach and the bowel.

3. *What were his verbal descriptions of the symptoms?*
He complained of 'pressure in the head', of 'feeling sick', of 'nausea',

of 'trembling', of 'being in the shit' and, sometimes, 'throwing up' before going to work. The first two symptoms recurred regularly during his working day.

4. *What were his life circumstances prior to the onset of the illness?*
He was a single man in his late twenties, with no current intimate relationship in his life, living alone, teaching mathematics and religion in a large all-boys second-level school. His parents were alive and residing in another county. His father was a secondary school principal and his mother was a deputy principal in a primary school. John was the eldest of two sons. His brother, two years younger, had refused to go to school from the age of eleven and, now, in his mid-twenties, was living at home and unemployed. He had been diagnosed with 'clinical depression' when he was fifteen and had been on antidepressant medication since that time. John was ashamed of his brother and, effectively, had no relationship with him. In school, all the students in John's mathematics classes were preparing for state examinations. He had also volunteered to take responsibility for several extra-curricular activities.

5. *Was any significant event due to occur?*
John constantly dreaded the next day, fearing that he might not be able to maintain his standards of perfectionism. During the weekends, he got little relief, because he would be preparing for the coming week and dreading the return to school on Monday.

6. *What was the current state of his inner terrain?*
Fear, worry and unrealistic expectations of himself were his daily inner experiences. He had a deep dread of failure and an addiction to success. He felt the need to prove himself all the time. He felt he had to be 'the best teacher' and get 'the best examination results'. Any falling short of these expectations exacerbated his fears. He had great worries about maintaining control in the classroom and he always made sure that he had more than enough work prepared in order to keep the students constantly busy. The religion classes were a nightmare for him because the students were not motivated and the likelihood of discipline problems was high. Not only did he

feel driven to prove himself to the school principal, other teachers and the students' parents, he also did not want 'to let down' his own parents. Because of his intense and enduring fears, he worked and worked to maintain success and people's approval. His whole life revolved around his teaching. The mornings were his most trying times, as he dreaded the day ahead. His symptoms of nausea and trembling added to his distress because he feared others would notice them.

7. *What was the present state of his external world?*

The following were key external circumstances in his current life:

- Tranquillizers three times daily; daily medication for high blood pressure.
- Living alone.
- Responsible for mathematics examination classes.
- Responsible for some classes on religion.
- Voluntary responsibility for several extra-curricular activities.
- High-achieving parents.
- Brother who had 'dropped out' of his academic studies and was diagnosed with endogenous depression.
- Went home most weekends.
- Worked long hours each evening preparing classes.
- Poor diet.
- No friends.
- No interests outside of teaching.
- No hobbies.

8. *What were his symptoms making him do?*

The illness brought attention to the fact that there was something wrong in his life; it got him to give some care to himself – it got him physically to attend to the pressure in his head, stomach and bowel. He was also compelled to lie down when he felt pressure in his head, to release the pressure in the bowel through diarrhoea, and to take tranquillizers for his overwhelming anxiety.

9. *What did the illness allow him to stop doing?*

The illness meant it was impossible for him to maintain the intense pressure he was putting on himself to be 'the best teacher' and, thereby, stopped him from 'doing too much'. The illness also stopped him from 'keeping everything down', because it forced him to seek professional help.

10 and 11. *What threats/disharmonies was the self signalling through the illness? What domain of self-expression was being flagged as having been repressed?*
In this young man's case the illness spoke so eloquently, through metaphor and analogy, of the conditions for love and recognition which, tragically, he had learned from his childhood days:

- His need to be 'a-head' of his colleagues.
- The high pressure he felt compelled to put himself under.
- His utter dependence on success for his 'vitality' (blood being the vital life medium).
- His intense fear of criticism, failure, rejection and abandonment – all the experiences he had learned to dread and 'could not stomach'.

12 and 13. *What realization was the self trying to bring forward? What real actions were being signalled as necessary for the young man's wholeness?*
Through the illness, John was attempting to bring into the open his deservingness of unconditional love; his worthiness of visibility, recognition and attention – not for being 'the best', not for reflecting well on his parents, not for living up to expectations, but simply for the fact of his unique presence in the world. The real actions that needed to be taken were concerned with finding love, understanding, compassion and acceptance for himself, and, thereby, creating the safety that would allow him to find separateness from his parents and brother and live life for himself in freedom.

A Story of Uncovering the Intentions of Irritable Bowel Syndrome

Kate's story, below, of irritable bowel syndrome reveals how it can take a long time for us to find the place of safety that will enable us to explore the intentions underlying whatever illness emerges in our life.

Kate was in her early forties when she came for help for irritable bowel syndrome, a condition that had started in her early teenage years. She described her symptoms as 'severe cramps in my gut'. The onset of symptoms usually occurred when getting ready to go to a social function. She said: 'At times the cramps would become unbearable and I would have to lie down until they abated.' In spite of medical interventions, these cramps had continued throughout her life, mostly when socializing or when preparing for academic examinations. It emerged that, from a very early age, this woman's individual lifestyle was metaphorically 'cramped' in her relationship with her mother, who commanded conformity to her own perfectionist ways and harshly condemned any falling short of her standards. Kate's family was also of the kind where 'children should be seen but not heard'.

Listening to the phrases commonly used by Kate gave clues as to the meaning of her illness. She talked often, for example, of finding something 'hard to digest' or 'hard to swallow', and used phrases such as 'that stuck in my throat', or 'I can't stomach criticism'.

It emerged in her exploration of the meaning of her illness that the core issue for Kate was her terror of reliving in social situations the rejection she had experienced in her childhood home. The irritable bowel symptoms were the metaphorical representation of that deep dread. The symptoms, by forcing her to lie down and pay heed to what was happening to herself, in a substitute way got her to *stop* focusing on how others were going to receive her and *compelled* her to attend to herself. In spite of the cramps, Kate rarely avoided the social outing – this would have exposed her to possible criticism from family members – but, at least, the symptoms 'gave her permission' to give herself some comfort before going out.

Kate recognized the wisdom of her symptoms and realized the repressions of her self-expression that they were signalling – the repression of her worthiness of living life for herself, rather than taking her cues for living from others; the repression of the rightness of being there for herself, rather than being there to measure up to her parents' expectations; the repression of her worthiness of non-judgemental relating. The real actions that Kate took on were concerned with the kind of unconditional parenting of herself that neither of her parents had been able to provide. As she progressed down the road of being lovingly attentive to herself, attentive to 'what her own gut told her' about how to live life, attentive to her own judgement of things, attentive to 'following her own star', Kate's symptoms began significantly to reduce.

Kate's journey, however, was far from easy. As is often the case, she had experienced, over the years, other symptoms along with the irritable bowel syndrome, including gastric reflux, teeth grinding and an underactive thyroid. These too, Kate recognized, had metaphorical meaning – for her the gastric reflux had something to do with the 'acidity' of emotional rejection; the teeth grinding was representative of how her sense of self had been ground down; and her underactive thyroid was the means by which she could allow herself to slow down and be less over-active.

A Story of Uncovering the Intentions of Tinnitus

Andrew's story of tinnitus, below, highlights the importance of the context of one's life history in uncovering the intentions of illness. Andrew was a man of middle age, highly successful in the performance arts, who 'suddenly' developed what he described as 'this ringing in my ears'. These symptoms began at a time when he was in a place of blaming and castigating himself for not pursuing a position he had really wanted. The hypothesis was put to him that the ringing in his ears might represent the internal verbal thrashing he was giving himself, and might be signalling the need to listen to how he treated himself and be less alert to what others thought of him. It emerged that the tinnitus had forced him to withdraw from the bulk of his current very heavy workload and allowed him to spend some time reflecting on how life was for him.

Initially, Andrew was dubious that his symptoms had meaning and intention, but gradually he began to make connections for himself between the resounding hollowness of his own interior life and his father beating him around the head when he was a child – which he remembered as causing a 'ringing in my ears'. The tinnitus was a metaphor for him of the 'emotional noise' of violence, harshness, criticism and ridicule that he had experienced as a child. He described his sense of self as there being 'nothing inside', as a 'great void; a big empty hangar'. The tinnitus appeared to be signalling this inner void and alerting him to the need for him to reclaim his self, to establish solidly his own unique place in the world. As his exploration progressed, and as he began to be more strongly there for himself, he slowly began to experience a sense of inner fullness and an inner solidity and, at the physical level, the tinnitus also began to disappear.

A Story of Uncovering the Intentions of Cancer

Cancer has become the dreaded disease of our time. Because cancer is an illness that provokes great fear, it can be difficult for the person experiencing the disease to accept it as having compassionate and creative intention; a not uncommon reaction to the suggestion that it has meaning being, 'Are you telling me that I brought this on myself?' But there is 'no enemy within' and the self creates a serious illness when there is a grave issue at stake – when its presence is under great threat. The purpose of the self is not to bring on death or to endure pain, but to hold wholeness in a powerful, albeit substitute, manner. This is illustrated in the story of a young woman with terminal cancer with whom one of the authors had the privilege to work.

Jean had been sent by her GP for psychological help. At the time of her first visit, she had been given one month to live. During the session, she posed a heart-wrenching question: 'Why is it that it is only since I got the cancer my mother and father have told me for the first time that they loved me?' Why indeed? The query, 'What did the illness do for her that was not safe for her to do in a real and direct way?' is poignantly answered by her own question – the illness got her the open expression of love from her parents. She remembered that, as a child, her parents were constantly arguing and fighting; she particularly recalled the absence of any warmth and affection from both parents – no hugs, embraces, no holding, no loving words, no affirmation. At times she used to leave her home in a distraught state and go to a nearby beach, where she would pick up a small, smooth stone, place it in the middle of her palm, and roll it around for hours on end. Her therapist called the pebble her touchstone – symbolizing the heart of stone she met in each of her parents, and the little comfort she derived from holding it. The stone was her very poor substitute; it was inevitable that a more powerful substitute would emerge.

She lived for six months after her first session and told on the eve of her death that those six months were the happiest in her bleak life – she spoke of having learned to receive love and to show love. When asked how she felt about dying, she said she saw it 'as the space between the in- and the out-breath'. It was sadly ironic that this young woman, in her early twenties, who had not been touched by love until her final months, had so profoundly touched this author's life.

Applying the thirteen-query process to this young woman's illness uncovers deeply poignant and moving answers:

1. *What was the nature of the presenting symptoms?*
Jean had cancer that had metastasized throughout the body and a prognosis of one month to live.

2. *Where in the body were the symptoms located?*
The primary location was the lower abdomen.

3. *What were her verbal descriptions of her symptoms?*
She described her condition as: 'I have terminal cancer with only one month to live.' She spoke too about having had 'some awful feeling stuck down in the pit of my stomach for years'.

4. *What were her life circumstances prior to the onset of the illness?*
The answer to this query has been outlined above; it is a story of a loveless upbringing, of abject loneliness and emptiness, of a situation where any show of feelings was dismissed, ignored, laughed at or punished.

5. *Was any significant event due to occur?*
The tragic answer to this query was her impending death.

6. *What was the current state of her inner terrain?*
What emerged in the early sessions with her was an absence of any emotion – be it anger, sadness, fear, rage, love, joy, excitement. What was particularly distressing was that she had a fixed smile that did not alter, whether she was talking about the emotionless experiences growing up, the medical treatments she had undergone, or the fact that she was terminally ill. She was also perfectionist in everything she did – a substitute means of eliminating the possibility of criticism and rejection.

7. *What was the present state of her external world?*
The key circumstances were:

- High doses of morphine to control the pain
- Living at home with her parents
- Waiting to die.

8. *What were her symptoms making her do?*
The cancer, and its location, brought attention to the loveless life she had undergone and elicited what she herself described as each of her parents saying for the first time in her life that they loved her. In her time in therapy, she touched into all the sadness and rage, into her need for love and attention that she had buried in the pit of her stomach for years. The symptoms also meant that she had to attend to her stomach and physically nurture herself. In the therapeutic relationship, she began to nurture herself emotionally and to find the safety to receive and give love.

9. *What did the illness allow her to stop doing?*
The illness meant she had to stop pleasing others, stop her extreme

efforts to get everything right, and stop ignoring her own sacred presence.

10 and 11. *What threats/disharmonies was the self signalling through the illness? And what domains of self-expression were being flagged as having been repressed?*

In this young woman's case, the illness spoke so powerfully, through metaphor and analogy, of the depths of harsh abandonment and of early and persistent emotionless relationships. The repressions symbolized by her illness were: to never look for love; to keep all feelings deeply buried; and never to betray her inner turmoil – to keep a smile on her face.

12 and 13. *What realization was the self trying to bring forward? What real actions were being signalled as necessary for her wholeness?*

The realization that came forward was of her immense lovability and her worthiness of receiving and giving love. The actions that emerged as being necessary for her were to reach out, directly and openly, for the love she deserved, and to express her love to herself and to others, in the knowledge of the difference her love made in the world.

A Story of Uncovering the Intentions of Heart Disease

It is curious that although heart disease is the more common killer disease, there is less protective resistance to considering its possible intentions than there is in the case of cancer. This phenomenon may be owing to the fact that there is common recognition of the heart as the organ that represents love. The human heart can, apparently, last for 400 years but in many men it is destroyed within forty to fifty years! There is acceptance of the notion that men can often 'bypass' their hearts, that they can often 'block' the emotion of love, that they may require 'open-heart surgery' to bring attention to their dire need to love and be loved.

The present authors have worked with several high-level businessmen who developed blocked arteries that required surgical interventions. For example, Trevor, an international businessman, spent most of his time travelling from country to country by plane, train and car. His marriage had failed and he hardly knew his children. The stress and intensity of his work had provoked concern among some of his friends, who warned him: 'If you keep up this pace of work, you'll give yourself a heart attack!' Trevor responded: 'I won't get a heart attack; I'm the one who gives heart attacks!' Indeed, the latter was true, but his friends' warning also proved to be true. Luckily for Trevor, his cardiologist recognized 'the absence of heart qualities' in this man's repertoire of means of relating to others and suggested he seek help.

In following the thirteen-query process of investigating the possible intentions of his heart attack, the answers summarized below began to emerge for Trevor:

1. *What was the nature of the presenting symptoms?*
Trevor had just undergone a triple bypass heart operation.

2. *Where in the body were the symptoms located?*
His symptoms were located in the heart.

3. *What were his verbal descriptions of the symptoms?*
Trevor spoke matter-of-factly about the 'blocked' arteries, and the necessity of having a bypass operation.

4. *What were his life circumstances prior to the onset of the illness?*
His life circumstances included: a relentless and heartless pursuit of success; a marriage that had failed and had ended in separation; very infrequent contact with his children; a life dominated by work.

5. *Was any significant event due to occur?*
He was extremely anxious about being able to return to work as soon as possible and feared any delays.

6. *What was the current state of his inner terrain?*
His preoccupation with being successful originated in childhood. His father 'did not tolerate fools gladly' and used physical violence and harsh criticism to motivate his son to be 'top of the class'. He learned that success reduced the emotional threats of heartless abandonment and he put enormous pressure on himself to measure up to his father's unrealistic expectations. His mother provided no comfort,

failing to champion him in the face of his father's aggression and was herself emotionless in her parental relationship with him. He was obsessed with being the best in his profession. When he came to therapy, the heart disease had not yet reduced his obsession with work and success. What he wanted from therapy was help to get back to work as soon as possible.

7. *What was the present state of his external world?*
He lived alone and was without support from family of origin, his ex-wife or his children. He was prepared to follow any therapeutic regime that would speed up his recovery and his return to work. His high anxiety about financial worries and an early return to work was leading to insomnia and difficulty in concentrating.

8. *What were his symptoms making him do?*
The 'blocked' arteries and the triple bypass operation at least had brought his attention to the need to attend to his heart, albeit only at the physical level. The symptoms and the aftercare following surgery compelled him to relax, rest, eat healthily and begin to exercise.

9. *What did the illness allow him to stop doing?*
The illness had effectively stopped him from pushing himself, and neglecting himself, in order to achieve success.

10. *What threats/disharmonies was the self signalling through the illness?*
The threats signalled by the blocked arteries were: 'having no heart for himself', and 'being highly blocked emotionally'. He had no consciousness that the heart qualities of love, nurturance, kindness, tenderness, empathy, compassion, ease and joy were as critical as the head qualities of drive, ambition, determination, order, assertion, and achievement. But, of course, these two sets of qualities are essential for well-being and balance.

11. *What domains of self-expression were being flagged as having been repressed?*
The 'blocked' arteries symbolically represented the major blocks to emotional expression and the expression of the need to love and be

loved. Sadly, Trevor had repeated his own childhood experiences with his own children by reproducing his father in himself.

12. *What realization was the self trying to bring forward?*

The realization being brought forward was how severely the absence of the heart qualities had blocked his maturity and the expression of the fullness of his true loving nature.

13. *What real actions were being signalled as being necessary for him?*

The actions required for Trevor were those very ones that his parents had not been in a position to provide – love, kindness, nurturance, warmth, affection, celebration. Gradually, as the realization deepened, he did find heart for himself, for his ex-wife, and for his children. His anxiety about returning to work was replaced by recognition of the greater importance of the 'heart work' that had been so neglected in his life. He decided not to return to the world of business and, following training, he went on to work in the field of psychotherapy.

8 Uncovering Intentions:
Childhood Illnesses

Intentions in Childhood Illness: A Matter for Adults

In the case of children, uncovering the intentions of any illness that occurs is a matter for the significant adults in the child's life; clearly this is not a process that a child would have the safety to pursue. The most significant adults in the child's life are, of course, the parents, but the parents may not always be the best able to assist the child in the necessary process and professional help may be required.

While uncovering the intentions of the child's illness is a matter that adults necessarily need to take on, it is a matter that is likely to prove quite difficult. The difficulty lies in the fact that only the child has the real information on his or her inner terrain and on the issues he or she is trying to bring into the light through his or her illness. Accordingly, the process for the adult is, in many ways, akin to detective work, involving the need to pick up clues, to make informed guesses, to form wise hypotheses. This process involves careful listening, close attention, mindfulness of what is happening in the child's life, awareness of the nature of the relationships with significant others in his or her life. As for adults, important information can be gained by paying heed to the metaphors that may be involved in the illness itself, in the location of the illness, in the language associated with that particular body part, and in the way that the child describes the symptoms he or she is experiencing. It is important not to jump to conclusions, and to check, in whatever way possible, with the child's own sense of things.

Again, as for adults, the contexts within which the child is living are very important – the contexts of home, school, clubs, friendship groups, local community. Home is a key context but it is not the only significant consideration. It is the adult who has to figure out what action is needed to resolve the hidden issue for the child, and it is the adult who, most likely, will have to carry out the action or at least guide and help the child to take whatever action is within his or her scope. Close examination of the child's life situations is crucial to initiation of the most appropriate action. Sometimes, of course – especially in the case of more minor ailments – the underlying intention may be relatively easy to uncover. For example, there might be no great emotional detective work involved in discovering why a child has started having stomach cramps in the morning at the start of a new school year, with a new teacher who has a reputation for being 'very cross'. Nevertheless, it has to be recognized that it is difficult enough for adults to carry out the process of uncovering intentions on their own behalf, never mind having to do it for another, and so it is important to have patience and consideration for yourself, and to be open to seeking outside help if necessary.

The difficulty of the process of uncovering the intentions of a child's illness is compounded by the fact that for any adult, but particularly for the parents, it is always distressing to witness a child being ill; a distress that is at its most acute if the child, tragically, has a life-threatening illness. In addition to witnessing the child's distress, the adults in the child's environment have the further challenge of examining their own ways of being with children, with themselves, and with other significant adults involved in the situation – for example, parents have to examine how they are relating to one another. It can be a very difficult reality to face, but it needs to be recognized that the intentions of the child's illness may very likely have something to do with the nature of the relationships with the significant adults in his or her life. The challenge of compassion for adults is to come into awareness of their own inner terrain and their own substitute responses. This is a difficult challenge, but it is crucial that the adults surrounding the child come into the open, loving place necessary to investigate the intentions of the illness on behalf of the child. This challenge can be taken up only in an environment of non-judgement, non-blame, compassion and understanding. Parents need to be honoured as always doing their best within the context of their own inner terrain and their level of safety.

Some Common Childhood Illnesses: Possible Intentions

Some of the more common illnesses manifested by children include enuresis, encopresis, abdominal pain, skin conditions, tonsillitis, infections, asthma, obesity, diabetes mellitus and food allergies.

One story of the intentions of enuresis has already been given (Chapter 3) but it is important to remember that each child's enuresis will have a unique meaning for that child and this meaning will become clear only if the life situations of the child are closely examined. What can be said for all cases is that enuresis (wetting) is about realizing – bringing into the light – in a substitute way what the child dare not express spontaneously and openly. Encopresis (soiling) may be a creative attempt by the self to bring the attention of adults to the 'shitty' situations that the child is enduring. Again, what precisely these situations are can be detected only by looking closely at the inner and outer contexts of the individual child's life.

Abdominal pain is often about some experience the child is 'not stomaching', but dare not speak about openly. Tonsillitis, a not uncommon childhood complaint affecting one of the body's defensive organs, may be a metaphorical representation of the child's not wanting to swallow the hurt of emotional rejection. Recurring infections may be the child's way of trying to draw attention to some invasion of his or her boundaries that is recurring in his or her life. Asthma, a particularly frightening childhood condition, can be associated with the suppression of spontaneous expression of the child's individuality and unique responses to situations, or with overwhelming pressure to meet unrealistic performance expectations on the part of parents. The occurrence of an asthmatic episode can draw attention in a substitute way to the suffocating nature of the parental relationship with the child. As is often the case when an asthmatic episode occurs, the parents rush with an 'inhaler' to relieve the child's physical trauma, and now the child has 'permission' to stop having to perform, or to stop being silent about his distress. However, unless there is realization of the underlying repression and the child is allowed to breathe his own life and not be at the mercy of parents' over-protection or dominance or unrealistic expectations, the asthmatic symptoms will, inevitably, recur. Childhood obesity, a condition that is increasing in frequency, can metaphorically represent 'weighty' matters that need attention. Food represents nurturance and it can frequently be the case that food becomes the substitute for the emotional nurturance of love. Unless real rather than substitute nurturance is provided, the obesity will continue to worsen. Sometimes, particularly in the case of pre-pubescent girls, obesity can be a creative cover for fear around sexual development. The source of the repression can be incidents of sexual invasiveness, the experience of which lies hidden and unspoken. Diabetes mellitus, an illness connected with blood sugar, may be a metaphor for the 'sweetness' of kindness or the 'sweetness' of love that may be tragically lacking in the child's life. The need to administer daily injections serves to bring attention and care to the child, albeit in a substitute manner. The real care being signalled as being needed through the illness is for the parents to have quality time with the child each day, to keep a warm eye out for his or her overall well-being, and to be active in ensuring that life is sweet for the child. Food allergies, frequent among children, can metaphorically represent reactions to particular behaviours of a parent. As already mentioned, food is a symbol for love and nurturance and it can be the case that the child attracts his or her parents' attention through the substitute means of being allergic to certain foods. The allergy keeps the parents' attention on the child because there has to be close watch that he or she does not eat the 'taboo' food. The resolution lies in the parent realizing the underlying real need and paying a lot more attention to the provision of the real food of life – unconditional love.

Abdominal Pain: A Story of Uncovering its Intentions

A mother contacted one of the present authors about her six-year-old son, who was experiencing tummy pain. The mother explained that when the child had first complained some four months previously, she had brought him to the family doctor. The doctor duly examined the child's abdomen and could find no obvious physical cause for the child's pain. Nonetheless, he prescribed medication, on the basis that maybe the child had a low-grade infection, and recommended that the child stay out of school until the prescribed course of medication was completed. On the morning following the ending of the course of medication, the mother went to the child's bedroom, clapped her hands playfully and said: 'Seán, wake up now and get ready for school.' The child moaned and complained, 'But Mummy, my tummy is sore.' The mother reacted and crossly declared: 'Up now. Remember what the doctor said – there is nothing wrong with your tummy.' With that, the child threw himself out of the bed, vomited and began to bang his head against the bedroom door. Mother became alarmed and quickly reassured the child that he did not have to go to school. Eventually, the child calmed down and when she had returned him to his bed, she wisely asked: 'Seán, why don't you want to go to school?' The answer was prompt and spontaneous: 'Teacher shouts.' Here now we see what is 'sore' for the child – the emotionally threatening behaviour of a teacher shouting at children. The issue that needed to be immediately addressed was the child's response to the teacher's shouting – abdominal pain, vomiting and head-banging. (The issue of why the teacher is shouting is a separate one and not to be confused with the child's illness response.)

In attempting to uncover the intentions of the child's abdominal pain, of the thirteen queries involved in the process, the six essential queries in this case are:

- What is the child doing through the abdominal pain that he is not safe to do directly and consciously?
- What is the abdominal pain allowing the child to stop doing?

- What self-esteem aspect of the child's inner terrain is being embodied?
- What is the 'realization' that the parent, or other care-giving adult, needs to make?
- What is the child's symptom attempting to draw the adult's attention to?
- What are the actions the parent, and other significant adults involved, need to take on behalf of the child in order to restore safety in a real way in his world?

In terms of the first of these essential queries, Seán's 'pain in my tummy' is the child speaking in a substitute way about the 'emotional pain' he is experiencing. Clearly, it would be very threatening for him to voice his fear to the teacher and to let her know that her shouting is affecting his well-being. Children are very clever; they know when it is safe and when it is unsafe to talk. The question arises: why did he not feel safe to tell his mother or father about the threatening situation? It was only in the situation when his mother was threatening to force him to go to school and was panicked by his reactions of vomiting and head-banging that she provided the safety for him to voice his distress by asking him why he didn't want to go to school.

It emerged in therapy that the mother herself was very passive and, as a consequence, could not provide an empowering model for her child in his school world. Even after the child told her about the distressing situation at school, her response was to phone Parentline (a telephone help-line), rather than to high-tail down to the school and resolve the situation with the teacher in question. Unfortunately, she was advised: 'Yes indeed, do go down to the school, ask to see the child's teacher, but don't mention the teacher's shouting.' She was further advised to say to the teacher that the child was not feeling well at the moment and to request that, when he returned to class, she would keep a special eye out for him. This advice fed the mother's passivity and she duly complied, because it posed little risk for her.

Of course, because the shouting was not addressed openly and directly, the teacher continued in the same aggressive vein with the children in the classroom. On his return to school, and on re-encountering the teacher's shouting, the child's pain intensified and was followed by another spell of absence. Ten weeks later he had not returned to school. Clever child!

What about the father in this case? Like many fathers, he left the responsibility of parenting to the mother. He was under the impression that the child was having recurring infections; the mother, in her own insecurity, had not told him about the school situation for fear that he would go to the school and aggressively challenge the teacher – passivity can result in as much neglect of a child's welfare as can aggression.

With regard to the second essential query, the pain created by the self was effective in allowing the child to stop going to school, the environment that was posing such threats to his well-being.

With regard to the third query, the self-esteem issue in the child's inner terrain was the repression of what he was feeling and experiencing, and the mother's unwitting complicity in this repression through keeping the matter hidden. Children have a right to a climate of safety within each of the worlds they inhabit – home, classroom and school – but to voice openly that right is very threatening for children without the support of unconditionally loving relationships with the significant adults in their lives.

The realization – the fourth query – that the child's pain was crying out for was that his presence would be held unconditionally both in the classroom and in the home. It might seem, in this case, that it was the teacher's behaviour that was the main cause of the disharmony in the child's world, but, in truth, the child was not being held unconditionally by his mother or father either. If the child had been held with safety in the home, then he would have openly voiced his distress and his parents would have acted maturely to restore safety to his school world.

The wake-up call – the fifth query – was for the mother to face her substitute response of passivity, for the teacher to face her substitute response of aggression, and for the father to face his substitute response of maintaining a remote place in the family. The child's illness brought opportunities not only for the child to resolve in a real, rather than a substitute, way his own repression of his feelings and experiences, but opportunities also for the teacher, mother and father to resolve their repressions.

The real action – sixth query – that was required for the resolution of the child's abdominal pain was for the parents to go together to the teacher and talk *with* her about the threatening situation that had developed for their child in his school world. Seán's mother was very nervous of confronting the teacher and was fearful she would 'break down and start crying'. His father, on the other hand, was ready to 'tear the bitch apart'. The latter response makes it even more understandable why the child needed to embody, rather than openly express, his turmoil.

Eventually, the parents came to see that neither passivity nor aggression was going to resolve the situation. They also saw how these substitute responses on their part had made the world of home unsafe for their child. They were encouraged to talk with the teacher along open, direct and authentic lines: 'We have come to talk with you about Seán's absence from school, and the fact that he is terrified of your shouting in the classroom, suffers chronic abdominal pain when facing into coming to school, and has even vomited and head-banged. We need your help and support to make it safe for our child to return to school.' It can be seen that while this approach is assertive, it is non-judgemental and non-threatening. The teacher in question responded very openly to the parents, and reassured them that she would address the issue immediately and make definite efforts to welcome the child back to the classroom. Within weeks, the child was talking about his 'favourite teacher'.

Of course, not all difficult situations work out as well as this, but our experience is that no adult deliberately wants to threaten the well-being of a child and, when confronted in a mature way, is highly likely to respond positively. If the person does not respond, then further action is required until the intentions of the child's illness are addressed.

Adolescent Skin Conditions: Some Possible Intentions

Skin conditions are very common among teenagers – acne, boils and psoriasis being the most frequently experienced. The skin, the surface covering of the body, serves a dual purpose – separation and contact. On the one hand, it is the boundary of all that lies beneath in this particular human presence and, at the same time, it provides the most powerful means of human contact – the touch, the hug, the caress, the embrace, the stroking, the massage are all experienced through the skin. The skin serves a critical physical function by showing externally the level of well-being of our internal organs. At the psychological level, it can be a very powerful canvas for the self to express outwardly what is happening in the person's inner terrain. The skin can be seen as an amazing film screen that makes visible what has had to lie hidden. Whatever emerges on the skin – a boil, rash, goose pimples, redness, inflammation – its location is highly likely to be a metaphorical tool of the self to bring to the surface what lies hidden in the inner terrain.

Skin conditions that are attempting to reveal underlying emo-tional disharmonies will continue until the young person finds the safety to express and respond to existing unmet needs. In order to be able to respond to the intentions of any presenting skin condition, it is important to understand the context within which teenagers and young adults operate. Sadly, their world is often one where there is a strong expectation that one should 'put a brave face on things', and, in such a context, realization of the underlying intention is far less likely to occur than is the substitute response of 'covering up' the inner turmoil. This covering up can happen in two ways – at the physical level and at the emotional level. Powerful medical treat-ments for skin conditions and the highly creative, and expensive, cosmetic industry serve the physical cover-up very well. It has to be acknowledged that the cosmetic industry can reduce human suf-fering and create space for individuals who are afflicted to go beneath the skin and deal with the deeper emotional issues. It is very difficult, particularly in a culture that puts so much emphasis on 'the body beautiful', to talk about your inner fears and insecurities when you are covered with spots, or rashes, or when you blush very easily. The physical treatments help individuals 'not to lose face', but encouragement from medical and cosmetic practitioners to those afflicted to 'save their skins' at the psycho-social level would be a very significant addition to their comprehensive care.

Behind all the creative attempts to 'cover up', what frequently 'breaks out' in the skin of the young person is the very real and painful issue of the repression of love for themselves, particularly their physical selves. It is sad that there are so few individuals – young or old – who feel confident about their physical appearance; a common protective response being to find all kinds of external substitute ways of finding physical acceptance – the facial, the face-lift, the false tan, the striving for the 'six-pack' muscle tone. All such substitutes are necessary because they make living bearable until the person comes into a place of 'being beautiful', rather than 'looking beautiful'. The young people may still want to enjoy the pleasure that cosmetics and style can offer, but it is crucial that they are not dependent on them for their sense of self, that they understand that it is not clothes that makes the man or woman, and that they are comfortable in their own skins.

Acne

While the 'cover-up' has its place, it is important that young people with recurring skin conditions find the comprehensive care that provides the emotional security needed to discover what is really 'getting under their skin'. Acne, for example, while its physical cause may lie with hormonal imbalance, may be a metaphorical representation of the difficult dilemma of, on the one hand, wanting to make physical, sexual and emotional contact with another and, on the other hand, having a lack of confidence and a fear of rejection. Since the skin is the very organ by which we make contact, the location of symptoms in the skin can give important clues as to the hidden disharmonies in the young person's inner terrain. In terms of uncovering the intentions of acne – and these will be unique for each young person experiencing the condition – the critical questions are:

- What could the young person be trying to bring forward through the acne that is not safe to do directly and consciously?
- What is the acne allowing the young person to stop doing?
- What self-esteem aspect of the young person's inner terrain is being embodied?
- What is the 'realization' that needs to occur?
- What are the actions required on the part, or on behalf, of the young person in order to find confidence and fearlessness?

The first query is concerned with what it is that lies hidden that needs to be openly talked about. But it can be very unsafe for young people to talk openly about their chronic lack of confidence and shyness around those for whom they have a strong sexual and physical attraction. The acne acts as a substitute, in that they can now talk about something that is bothering them; they can talk, for example, about hating their spots. They are not talking about the real issue but, nonetheless, there is a chance now that some astute adult may 'spot' the real issue that needs to be brought to the surface and resolved.

In terms of the second question, the acne gives an 'excuse', a way out of taking the risk of making a move on the person to whom he or she is attracted, and, thereby, eliminating the possibility of feared rejection.

In regard to the nature of the particular repression that is being manifested – question three – this can only be truly discovered when there is sufficient safety for the young person to allow a compassionate parent, or care professional, or indeed a friend, into his or her inner terrain. It is never wise for anybody, professional or otherwise, to assume that you can tell what the hidden issues are for another; such assumption, or indeed any advice-giving, serves only to create unsafety in the relationship, and exacerbates the young person's inner turmoil and its outer skin manifestation.

In terms of the actions required – question five – there is a serious need for the significant adults in young people's lives to help them find effective ways of talking out their confidence difficulties, rather than having to talk through their skin. When young people do talk, it is important that they be guided and supported in the ways of coming into inner confidence and security. Resolution of these inner issues is, of course, a long-term process; in the meantime, it is important that young people can avail of effective physical treatments for the acne so that they may avoid the painful embarrassment and hurt that can often accompany the condition.

Childhood Infections: Some Possible Intentions

Infection is one of the most common and most basic aspects of the disease process within the human body. Most of the symptoms that present themselves in acute form are inflammations of one kind or another, from colds at one end of the continuum to glandular fever and lung infections at the other end. It is our experience that, in many cases, inflammation in young people is an unresolved conflict that has taken a physical form. This is not surprising in the context of a world in which adults, rather than treating conflict as the creative force it is, instead do their utmost to avoid it. The young person, unconsciously recognizing the threats to open expression of the conflict, attempts to work through the inner disharmony, the inner 'burning issues', by the substitute means of inflammation at the physical level. When young people transfer their conflicts to the physical level of inflammation symptoms, at least the conflict is being symbolically represented and attention is brought to the need to cool down matters, even if it is only the physical discomfort that is being cooled. The inflammation gets the parent, or other adult, who may be the source of the young person's inner conflict, to make efforts to reduce 'the fever' and to attend to the child without the distraction of other matters. The young person is likely to be prescribed an antibiotic by a medical practitioner, this acting as a temporary and substitute means of reducing the 'temperature' of whatever it is that has been getting the young person 'hot under the collar', 'into a fever', or 'livid'.

The real action needed is the creation of safety and the provision by significant adults of the mature expression of conflict that, while non-threatening of others, nevertheless calls a spade a spade. Young people can learn from adults that conflict is always about the person who is experiencing it: when inner conflict is projected outwards, it blames either individuals or social systems; and when it is introjected, the blame is put on oneself. When conflict is either projected or introjected, no resolution is possible and a physical representation is now likely to emerge. Young people require help to see that when conflict is owned as being about yourself, you have the possibility of openly expressing your blocked needs and of seeking ways to meet those needs, without in any way jeopardizing the well-being of others.

The significant adults surrounding a young person experiencing recurring inflammations could help greatly by considering the following questions:

- Is there conflict going on in or outside the home that the young person may be experiencing and internalizing? For example, is the young person being bullied by peers at school. Does the young person frequently witness verbal and/or physical hostility from a parent or between parents?

- Are there issues around the young person's concept of self that demand addressing? For example, does the young person hate his or her physical appearance; has he or she been compared to a 'more handsome/beautiful' sibling; is there a fear of sexual expression?

- Am I, as an adult, addressing my own conflicts? For example, do I, as a parent, need to examine my own preoccupation with the 'body beautiful'? Do I have difficulty with physical and emotional closeness?

- Do I, as an adult, need support to resolve my own conflicts or to take action to resolve my child's conflicts?

Glandular Fever

A relatively common infection experience among teenagers is glandular fever – the usual symptoms being sore throat, swollen glands and extreme tiredness. In our work with young people with this condition, we have noticed certain psycho-social features, such as a 'bottling up' of grief around troubled family relationships and the over-exhausting of oneself in the attempt to keep everyone happy. The location of symptoms in the throat can symbolically represent the swallowing down of the family 'sores' and the swollen glands can represent the swollen river of bottled-up feelings. The tiredness can serve the very powerful purposes of being forced to take a break from the endless task of keeping everyone happy and being faced with the necessity to attend to self. Resolution lies in the young person being enabled to take up the one and only responsibility that he or she can actually carry out – responsibility for one's own self and one's own actions – and being supported in allowing others to resolve their own life difficulties.

A Story of the Intentions of Childhood Heart Disease

The following story of a child diagnosed with 'a leaking heart valve', and needing surgical intervention, brings stark attention to the need to approach illness from both the medical perspective of looking for causes and the psycho-social perspective of looking for intentions. (The story was related, and the intentions of the illness were uncovered, only in adulthood.)

At the onset of the illness, Veronica was twelve years old, the youngest in a family of five, with one sister and three brothers. Three years previously her father had died after a long illness. Her deeply bereaved and distraught mother was left with debts and her five children to rear and educate on her own. Her mother was a primary school teacher who, despite her tremendous loss, was determined to give all her children the best education. Following the father's death, there had been much disruption in the family: the oldest boy had to drop out of college for a year, and for the sake of educational needs, the two younger boys went to live with uncles close to 'good' schools, and, shortly afterwards, Veronica's sister – to whom she was very close – also left home for boarding school.

Veronica keenly felt the loss of her father and of her siblings, in particular her sister. While these losses might have had some acknowledgement, what was not appreciated was that the child had also lost the 'heart' of her mother – to grief, pressures of responsibility, and her own anxieties. The temporary return home of her oldest brother served somewhat to ease the blows for some time, as he effectively took over the father role towards Veronica. At the time of onset of the symptoms – early summer – Veronica herself was due to leave for boarding school in the autumn, at which time her mother would then be living on her own at home. Veronica was in no way emotionally ready, or secure enough, to leave her mother and her home. Her heart disease presented itself in symptoms of palpitations, which she could feel in every part of her body from 'head to toe', in chest pains, in a sense of great tiredness, and in strong and very disturbing 'feelings of unreality', which she tried desperately to assuage through eating.

Metaphorically, the 'leaking heart' represented the many 'heart' losses that Veronica had already experienced and was due to further experience. The events in the past and the events anticipated for the future led to the self creating an illness with the substitute intention of getting some attention for her heartache and dread of a further disruption of relationships. The subconscious hope was that somebody would detect the psychological threats to her well-being. It would have been very threatening for Veronica to speak directly to any family member – most of all her mother – about her fears and losses. She wanted to be the 'good girl', who was 'so brave', and who did not add in any way to her mother's grief and anxiety. Her mother was already deeply traumatized and her surrogate-father brother was beginning to rebel against an overload of responsibility.

In Veronica's exploration as an adult of the context of the illness, it emerged that there was something of a taboo on expressing emergency feelings within the family, and there was a strong, if unspoken, pressure among the children to protect the mother as much as possible. The wisdom for Veronica was to find a way to say what needed to be said, but in a way that would not further threaten the key relationships in her life.

Although, from the start of her symptoms, surgery had been identified as being necessary, the operation had not been scheduled immediately because of her very poor physical condition. The medical prescription was for complete rest until such time as she could sustain surgical procedures. All the family, friends and neighbours rallied round Veronica, providing care, tenderness, attention and entertainment – she was the centre of attention. Three months later, within days of the planned surgery, all symptoms disappeared.

Veronica remembers the joy of receiving so much loving care, but she also remembers that she knew her condition was putting her in the grave danger of having to leave home and the dreaded prospect of an operation. Very importantly, it had been decided that, given her health situation, she would stay at home for the coming year and boarding school would be postponed. Her medical carers were amazed at her sudden 'recovery', a recovery that her family – especially her mother – put down to a miracle. From the psychological perspective, it can be seen that the illness had served its purpose of getting attention for her heart losses and of postponing further disruption of her relationship with her mother, and its prolongation would have proved counterproductive.

The key questions in uncovering the intentions of Veronica's heart disease are:

- What did the illness do for her that was not safe for her to do consciously?
- What did the illness stop her from doing that she could not do directly?
- What repression was the illness attempting to bring into the light?
- What open, conscious actions did the child need to have taken for her?

In regard to the first question, the illness spoke eloquently, though covertly, of all her heart losses.

In regard to the second question, what stopped following the onset of her symptoms was the lack of attention to her inner grief state, albeit the attention was given to the illness symptoms rather than directly to her psychological distress. But this was the only way for the child to let it be known that she needed attention.

The repression being highlighted by the illness was the taboo around emotional expression, particularly of emergency emotions, that her family, particularly her mother and her father, found threatening.

The conscious actions that the child needed to have taken were the expression of unconditional love, and the encouragement and support to express her inner emotional world. This outcome was not achieved by the illness at the time, and it was only later in adult life that Veronica found the safety for open, real emotional expression and for strong, firm action on behalf of her well-being.

9 Finding Compassionate Caring

Compassionate Caring: Whose Responsibility?

As has been emphasized throughout this book, when any one of us becomes ill, we deserve to have all the stops pulled out in our care. Comprehensive care means that, alongside the physical treatment, we also get the help we need to address the psycho-social intentions underlying the illness. In other words, wholeness becomes as important as alleviation or the cure of physical symptoms. You will have seen from the previous chapters that although uncovering the intentions of the self in illness can sometimes be fairly straightforward and can be a journey you embark on by yourself, there are other times of serious or life-threatening illness when the process can be quite profound, involving deeply rooted issues stretching back to childhood, and accompanied by strong and deep-seated emotions. In the latter, professional help is likely to be required. The question then arises as to who best can provide the person who is ill with the professional care needed in the uncovering process. At present, when you become ill, the professionals you come in contact with will almost always belong to the medical arena. Clearly, we could not expect it to be part of the brief of medical professionals to embark on the process of uncovering the psycho-social intentions of the illness with the person in their medical care. The accompanying of the person in the psycho-social processes of illness needs to be in the charge of professionals with a psychology/psychotherapy background who have a particular interest and specialized training in the field.

While medical professionals will have one particular brief and psycho-social professionals will have another in their relationships with the person who is ill, it is incumbent on everybody in the environment surrounding the person to maintain the kind of compassionate, caring, understanding interactions that will create safety. This kind of relationship is within the ken of *everybody*, regardless of profession, and indeed is a *responsibility* that is incumbent on everybody – medical, psychological and social professionals, administrative staff, family members and friends.

Compassionate Relating: What Does It Involve?

Compassion is part of our true nature but, depending on the state of our inner terrain, we may or may not be in a position to act compassionately in an open and conscious manner. It has to be recognized that *we all* – doctor, patient, psychologist, client, parent, child – go through the same human processes and, accordingly, it is the person who can discover and resolve his or her own repressions who is in the best position truly to help another. Any one of us who is out of contact with our inner world, and who lacks the understanding that our inner terrain, moment by moment, determines our every word and action, can unwittingly create threats for others around us. The starting point for care of another is care of yourself. The challenge, then, for anyone involved with someone who is ill is to become more conscious of his or her own inner terrain and substitute responses, and to seek resolution of his or her own issues so that he or she may be able to respond in real, rather than substitute, ways towards the person experiencing the illness. There may be times when taking up this challenge requires help from another. It is important that we do not put unrealistic expectations on ourselves in regard to this inner journey; all we need is to be 'good enough' care-givers.

We have listed below what seems to us to be some of the central qualities of compassionate relating; see from your own experience what other qualities you might want to add to the list. Bear in mind that these qualities are part of the self's natural way of being in the world and they emerge spontaneously when there is safety in the worlds you inhabit. If, in going through the list, you notice the absence of some of these qualities in the way you currently relate to others, it is important that you recognize this as a necessary defence against perceived threat on your part, and that, rather than judging yourself, you attempt to get underneath the defence so that the repression can be resolved and you can return to openness.

Key Qualities of Compassionate Relating

- Being non-judgemental.
- Being present to the other; actively listening.
- Being open to the other's difference from you.
- Being supportive of the other's attempts to find openness.
- Being considerate of the other's particular circumstances.
- Staying separate – knowing that your story and the other's story are separate issues and both have their own reality and their own truth.
- Being empowering of the other to live his or her own life according to his or her own light.
- Being understanding of the threats that can arise in the worlds we inhabit.
- Being gentle in your approach to the other.
- Being nurturing; conveying the other's worthiness of care.
- Recognizing the other as the 'expert' – and the only expert – in his or her own life.
- Being empathic towards the feelings of the other, knowing that they arise from the self and are there for the person's well-being.
- Being patient; knowing that the other's fears and vulnerabilities come from real experiences in his or her world.
- Being non-intrusive in the other's space; allowing the other to make his or her own sense of things, and make his or her own choices and decisions.
- Bearing witness to the emotions and experiences of the other, without imposing your own agenda.

Creating a Supportive Care Environment

The response to illness of others surrounding the person who is ill is a crucial consideration in the illness-journey undertaken. This is particularly true in the case of those involved in the care professions – medical, psychological and social. The responses of the care professionals to the presenting symptoms can be the determining factor in whether or not the illness is recognized for its substitute purpose and whether or not the person who is ill can discover the real actions that are being called for by the illness. Every professional in contact with the person who is ill, although he or she may not have a direct role in the process of uncovering intentions, has an important part to play in creating an environment supportive of the process. Any professionals, medical or psycho-social, who wish to provide comprehensive care need to understand that the person who is ill, like each one of us, is a creator, not a victim. It needs to be understood that the self has intention in the illness, the intention being to bring into the open the repressions of self-expression that have had to occur and that lie hidden in the person's inner terrain (see Chapter 3). Furthermore, it needs to be understood that the impetus of the self in illness is towards wholeness, pointing the way towards the real, conscious actions that are necessary to safeguard the person's well-being (see Chapter 1).

Symptoms are a passport into the domain of the professional helper, but it is the professional's level of understanding of the processes underlying the symptoms that will determine whether or not the necessary holistic therapeutic environment is created. The health-care professional who adopts the perspective of illness as meaningful and purposeful will naturally respond to the person who is ill as a wise creator who deserves to be involved in any discussions concerning his or her illness, so that he or she may be empowered to take responsibility for the resolutions needed. If the environment is of a nature where signs and symptoms of illness are seen as the enemy to be controlled, to be got rid of at all costs, then it is highly unlikely that the person who is ill will find the safety to appreciate and explore the wise substitute purpose of the illness. In such an environment, the health-care professional may reduce or eliminate the symptoms but will not be able to support the person who is ill to discover the deeper emotional afflictions that require urgent attention. Regardless of its cause – whether purely physical or psycho-physical – the implementation of a compassionate and holistic response to the illness is necessary.

Responding to illness as having psycho-social intention, rather than just as a physical occurrence, may, for some care professionals, involve a profound shift in perspective. The most powerful way to understand the meaning of illness, and to act from that under-standing, is for oneself to go through the thirteen-query process in regard to whatever illness may arise in one's own life. When you experience the meaning of the process for yourself, then you can genuinely accompany another when they need to embark on the same process. Appreciation of one's own wisdom, and compassion for oneself, gives rise to compassion and respect in relation to others.

Readiness to Assist in the Uncovering Process

While everybody in the environment surrounding the person who is ill has the responsibility to respond with compassion, and while all care professionals have the responsibility to provide the holistic approach that enables comprehensive care, there will be some pro-fessionals who will have the specific brief to assist the person in undergoing the psycho-social process involved in uncovering the intentions of the illness. In order to be ready to carry out this brief, the professionals concerned will need the support of appropriate training; the two key strands of appropriate training being explo-ration of relationship with self, and exploration of the nature of relationship with others.

Relationship with Self

The goal of this element of the training is increased self-reliance. Self-reliance provides the platform that enables you to stay separate, and thereby be able to accompany the other in whatever arises for him or her – in despair and hope, in ill health and well-being, in depression and joy. Paradoxically, it is in the attainment of our separateness that we find our essential solidarity with our fellow human travellers; in the words of Kahlil Gibran (Gibran, 1996), 'separateness is the basis for togetherness'. Self-possession provides the professional with the wherewithal to maintain compassion, understanding and consistency when faced with the often distressing substitute response of illness. Furthermore, when you are self-reliant, you are more likely to spot when you slip from a solid inner terrain; you will be able to apologize to the person who has sought your help and get back on the track of being present to the other person.

Since personal effectiveness lies at the heart of professional effectiveness, the training will need to provide opportunities for the trainees to explore their own inner terrains, their own repressions and their own substitute responses, including, in particular, times in their lives when illness has been the substitute response created by the self in the face of threats in their worlds (see Chapter 3). You will have seen from Chapter 2 the kind of safe holding we need in order to be able to give open, conscious expression in the different domains of expression available to the self – emotional, physical, sexual, intellectual, behavioural, social and creative. Sound training needs to provide opportunities for the trainees to become more conscious of the levels of safety that they have experienced in these different domains of self-expression, to identify the kinds of repressions that may have been necessary for them, and to find ways now in their own relationship with themselves of making it safer for them to find open, real self-expression.

In attempting to assist another in the process of uncovering the intentions of illness, a consciousness of your own substitute responses is crucial, so that you may not bring them into the space of the person who is ill. You will have seen in Chapter 3 that our various substitute responses may be categorized as acting-in, acting-out, addictions and embodiments. In an effort to provide some signposts for the discovery of one's typical substitute responses, we have listed below some of the more frequent substitute responses in the acting-in and acting-out and addictions categories (examples of embodiments have been given throughout the book). Bear in mind that the frequency, intensity and endurance of any particular substitute response are important barometers of the extent and depth of the underlying repressions. For example, if when you get enmeshed with another person's behaviour, your typical substitute response is to be sarcastic, it is useful to note how cruel are your cutting remarks, how long you go on with the sarcastic talk, and how long you have been engaging in this kind of behaviour. When you notice yourself reacting in any of the ways listed, it is important to maintain a compassionate stance towards yourself and to remember that your substitute responses arise from the experience of threat and the consequent disharmony in your inner terrain. Allow for the possibility that you, too, may need the assistance of somebody who can hold a compassionate space for you to discover the sources of your substitute responses.

Acting-out	*Acting-in*
Aggression	Passivity
Ridicule	Shyness
Cynicism	Timidity
Sarcasm	Nervousness
Arrogance	Anxiety
Superiority	Worry
Dominance	Self-criticism
Control	Self-deprecation
Violence	Avoidance
Rigidity	Aversion to risk
Impatience	Helplessness
Irritability	Fearfulness
Blaming	Tentativeness
Judgement	Perfectionism
Manipulation	Being a martyr
Volatility	Physical withdrawal
Carelessness	Over-protection

| Threats | Ingratiating |
| Prescriptions | Unsureness |

Substance and Process Addictions

Addiction to:
- alcohol
- drugs
- food
- sex
- work
- money
- possessions.

Nature of Relating with Others

When you are accompanying another in the process of uncovering an illness's intentions, it is important to bear in mind that the experience of the illness will always be particular to the individual involved. You will need to stay open to the person who is ill and be alert to the danger of seeing him or her through the lens of a theory – any theory simply represents the particular outlook on the world of the theorist. In truth, the only person who has the answer to the meaning of any particular incidence of illness is the person who is experiencing the illness. The professional helper's essential task is to create the compassionate environment that makes it safe for the person to express what, up to now, has not been safe to express. In working through the queries in the uncovering process, the essential matter to bear in mind is the contexts surrounding the person presenting with the illness symptoms. It is only by examining the inner and outer contexts of the person's life that the presenting illness will be discovered to have profound meaning and purpose (see Chapter 6). The appropriate timing for such a holistic exploration will need to be guided by the degree of acuteness of the person's illness and the level of urgency for medical attention.

In order to assist you in being reflective on the nature of your relating with others, we have identified below some of the key requirements for the creation of an effective therapeutic relationship. Here, we can only touch on what would need to be covered comprehensively in a sound training course. These requirements are in addition to the elements listed in the earlier section (p. 140) in regard to the creation of a compassionate environment.

Some Key Requirements in Creating an Effective Therapeutic Relationship

- Maintaining equality in the relationship.
- Being present to the other and present to yourself.
- Being an active, non-judgemental and non-interfering listener.
- Honouring and valuing the wisdom and creativity of the other person.
- Maintaining a stance of 'hypothesis' rather than 'certainty'.
- Being ready to discuss matters with the other.
- Seeking to empower, rather than 'rescue' or 'mind', the other.
- Being aware of your own feelings and experiences, and dealing with them in some other space, so that they are not brought into the space of the person who is ill.
- Ceding place to the other as the expert in his or her own life.
- Being non-directive; the other dictates the pace and the direction of the exploration.
- Staying calm while being emotionally genuine in the face of the other's distress.
- Being empathic towards and able to hold the strong emotions that often can emerge.
- Being aware and respectful of the depth of the processes involved and sensitive to the threats that underlie the substitute responses.
- Having a deep understanding of the metaphorical language of illness (and of other substitute responses), so that you can guide the person in the uncovering process.
- Being open to being creative in interpreting metaphorical language.

- Supporting the person in taking whatever action is within his or her level of safety.
- Maintaining patience at all times.

Being non-directive and recognizing the other as the expert in his or her own life does not mean there is no scope for making suggestions about what may be the deeper intentions of the presenting illness. But being non-directive does mean that, even when you feel you have spotted quickly the metaphorical nature of the symptoms, you put forward your sense of things only as hypotheses to be explored. It is for the person to say, for example, 'That makes sense to me'; 'That fits with what's going on in my life at the moment'; or 'That's not ringing any bell for me'. No matter how convinced you may be that you have seen through to the substitute purpose of the illness, it will do the person no good if you try to convince him or her that you are right. You need to be sensitive to the fact that sufficient safety may not yet be present for the person to come to the realization of his or her unconscious intentions, and to face the challenge involved in responding to possible intentions. Patience is crucial, along with acceptance of the other's stance at any particular time. Once you continue to be fully present to the other person, realization may very well come about for him or her.

You need to be ready to enter discussion with the person on the compassionate intention of the illness. Entering discussion does not in any way diminish your own knowledge and expertise, but it does recognize the fact that none of us can know another better than they know themselves. The illness is the other person's creation and it is for you to create the relationship that will make it safe for him or her to bring you into his or her inner terrain. If discussion does take place, you need to keep it at the level of exploring hypotheses and possibilities.

A stance of 'understanding' is very important. In the context of uncovering the metaphorical meaning of illness, the word 'understanding' has more connotations than it has in everyday language; here 'understanding' has the meaning of 'getting under the presenting stand of the person'. You will have seen in Chapter 5 how amazingly resourceful the self is in creating the metaphors and substitutes that will exactly represent what it is that lies hidden and that needs to be brought into the light. Essentially, the practice of understanding is the practice of not taking what is presented at face value but of following its lead to the deeper, more serious, hidden issues. The language of metaphor serves the purpose of giving voice to what really needs to be expressed but what, up to now, has been too risky to voice directly and consciously.

Being empathic is not about feeling sorry for the other. Being empathic means being able to accompany the other into his or her emotional world, and being able to bear witness to the powerful emotions that may be present. The word 'emotion' contains the word 'motion' and, indeed, emotion is always about movement: welfare emotions showing that current movement is conducive to well-being; emergency emotions showing that new movement is needed to address threats to well-being. Empathy provides the support for the person to take up the movement being called for by the specific emotion present. For example, anger comes from the self to provide the energy to take action on something that has become a block or an obstacle to one's development or progress in life. Sadness calls attention from the self to some blocked or unmet need and the action needed to meet that need. Depression invites a 'going down' into oneself, so that you may discover which repression is looking for open expression. Empathy involves recognizing that emotions arise from the self and are always concerned with one's well-being.

Bibliography

Bertherat, Therese and Bernstein, Carol (1988): *The Body Has Its Reasons,* London, Cedar Books.

Dethlefsen, Thorwald and Dahlke, M.D., Rudiger (2002): *The Healing Power of Illness,* London, Vega Books.

Groddeck, Georg (1977): *The Meaning of Illness,* New York, International Universities Press, Inc.

Lake, Frank (1996): *Clinical Theology,* London, Darton, Longman and Todd.

Maslow, Abraham (1954): *Motivation and Personality,* New York, Harper.

O'Connor, Dermot (2006): *The Healing Code,* Ireland, Hodder Headline.

Page, Christine (2005): *Frontiers of Health,* London, Rider

Page, Christine and Hagenbach, Keith (1999): *Mind Body Spirit Workbook, A Handbook of Health,* UK, C.W. Daniel Co. Ltd.

Siegel, Bernie (1986): *Love, Medicine and Miracles,* New York, Harper & Row.

Siegel, Bernie (1990): *Peace, Love and Healing,* London, Rider.

Totman, Richard (1979): *Social Causes of Illness,* London, Souvenir Press.

Winnicott, D.W. (1965): *The Maturational Processes and the Facilitating Environment,* London, Hogarth; Karnac (1990).